T5-AFU-452

★ ★ ★ ★ ★

GOVERNORS ON GOVERNING

Edited by Robert D. Behn

NATIONAL GOVERNORS' ASSOCIATION
Washington, D.C.

★

UNIVERSITY PRESS OF AMERICA
Lanham • New York • London

Copyright © 1991 by

National Governors' Association
444 North Capitol Street, Suite 250
Washington, D.C. 20001

University Press of America ®, Inc.
4720 Boston Way
Lanham, Maryland 20706

3 Henrietta Street
London WC2E 8LU England

All rights reserved
Printed in the United States of America
British Cataloging in Publication Information Available

Co-published by arrangement with
National Governors' Association

Portions of Governor Dick Thornburgh's essay are extracted
from "Crisis Management: Ten Key Lessons from the Three
Mile Island Experience." which originally appeared in
Public Affairs Review, © 1985 Public Affairs Council.
Such parts are reprinted by permisson.

Library of Congress Cataloging-in-Publication Data

Governors on governing / edited by Robert D. Behn.
        p.   cm.
   1. Governors—United States.   I. Behn, Robert D.
JK2447.G69   1990   353.9'1313—dc20   90-43216 CIP

ISBN 0–8191–7890–X (alk. paper)
ISBN 0–8191–7891–8 (pbk. : alk. paper)

The paper used in this publication meets the minimum requirements of
American National Standard for Information Sciences—Permanence
of Paper for Printed Library Materials, ANSI Z39.48–1984.

LIBRARY
ALMA COLLEGE
ALMA, MICHIGAN
★ ★ ★ ★ ★

Contents

★ ★ ★ ★ ★

Acknowledgments

This book is the product of governors themselves. It was made possible by sixteen governors who were willing to step back from the fray, look at their experience, and share their insights—in a very personal, rather objective, and highly provocative fashion. They did so as participants in the Gubernatorial Fellows Program at Duke University between 1984 and 1988. Each governor delivered a major address, conducted seminars, met with faculty, and talked with students over a two-day period. Their formal presentations are included as essays in this book.

The Gubernatorial Fellows Program is the flagship activity of The Governors Center at Duke University, launched in 1984 as an initiative of Terry Sanford, then president of Duke University and former governor of North Carolina, and financially supported by the National Governors' Association. The tasks of hosting the governors' visits, documenting their presentations, and editing their manuscripts were led by Robert D. Behn, the center's director and editor of this book. This process was overseen by Regina K. Brough, the center's executive director, with the assistance of Meret Keller and copy editor Robert Farris.

As the program sponsor, the National Governors' Association provided general support and encouraged the publication of this collection of essays, under the leadership of Raymond C. Scheppach and Barry L. Van Lare, NGA executive director and deputy executive director. Douglas P. Champion and Kelly Donley French of the NGA Office of State Services steered the project through publication in collaboration with Rae Young Bond and Gerry Rush Feinstein of the NGA Office of Public Affairs. Production assistance was provided by NGA staff members Linda A. Long, Virender S. Manocha, and Mark R. Miller. Dawn Detwiler, managing editor of

University Press of America, Inc., helped coordinate the publication process.

These essays are expected to contribute in a major way to understanding the state of the art of governing—for students and scholars of public leadership and management and for those who are given the rare opportunity to govern. For this legacy provided by our featured gubernatorial fellows, we are foremost and deeply grateful.

★ ★ ★ ★ ★

Introduction

Governors often claim that, except for the president of the United States, they have the best job in the world. Whether Democratic or Republican, liberal or conservative, all want to accomplish something significant, something unique during their years as governor. To many of them, states are the "laboratories of democracy." To students and scholars of government, the states might also be considered the "crucibles for governing."

Who better than governors to teach others about governing? Yet, most governors are too busy governing to take time to do so. The Gubernatorial Fellows Program at Duke University provides an opportunity for an incumbent governor to take a two-day respite from the state capital to deliver a formal presentation, conduct seminars, and talk informally about governing.

An average of four governors per year serve as gubernatorial fellows. This collection of essays is drawn from the presentations made by sixteen gubernatorial fellows from October 1984 through October 1988.

These governors were and continue to be considered leaders among their peers. They traverse the gubernatorial spectrum—geographically, politically, and philosophically. Their common bond is the governorship and their firsthand insights on "being there." Although their governing styles differ, common themes emerge.

This collection reflects the essential character of the contemporary American governor. Governors are optimists, activists, and federalists. They are optimistic about what state government can accomplish. They are activists who use the formal and informal powers of their office to realize their dreams and aspirations for their states. They are federalists who believe that state government plays an increasingly important role in the American intergovernmental system. Governors believe that states can and do improve and enrich the lives of citizens.

When approaching the task of governing, governors take the long view. Looking to the future, they create a vision of what can be done, then provide the leadership and management needed to fulfill that vision. They use their "bully pulpit" to build support, then devise strategies, and ultimately make it happen.

In their words—as in practice—governors emphasize results. Early in their term of office, they realize that they cannot accomplish everything. They must set priorities and focus their energies and resources. Some choose education. Others focus on jobs, or health, or the environment. All are expected to produce results.

Many forces constrain how governors govern—the roles that the states play in the intergovernmental system, the resources available to provide needed services, the institutional powers granted to a governor. These forces, and the challenges they pose, provide the essential "contexts for governing." We look at these contexts in Part One of this book.

Governor Charles Robb of Virginia focuses on the limits of scarce resources and on the difficulties in satisfying the demands of interest groups. Governor Michael Castle of Delaware deals specifically with fiscal constraints and how they can be transformed into opportunities. Governor Scott Matheson of Utah looks at the changing roles of federal, state, and local governments and the emerging diffusion of power to the states. Governor Richard Riley of South Carolina traces changes in the balance of power within the states, particularly between the executive and legislative branches. All point to enlightened leadership and management as the keys to gubernatorial success.

Therefore, to understand governing, it is important to understand the leadership and management roles that governors play. Seven essays on "gubernatorial roles" are clustered in Part Two of this book. Although some governors focus on leadership and others emphasize management, all recognize the importance of both.

Governor Lamar Alexander of Tennessee illustrates, through analogies, what governors do. Governors Madeleine Kunin of Vermont, John Ashcroft of Missouri, and Bob Graham of Florida focus on the leadership roles of governors, particularly the visions they provide for the future. Governor John Carlin of Kansas looks at communication as the key ingredient for both effective public leadership and administration. Governors Richard Celeste of Ohio and Victor Atiyeh of Oregon take a "CEO" perspective of the governorship, drawing parallels with the private sector and its business management approaches.

Understanding how governors view their roles and how they define leadership and management can help predict and explain their actions. The ways governors meet the challenges of their office and play their roles are best illustrated through case studies. The five essays in Part Three of this book provide candid autobiographical studies of "governors in action."

Governor Booth Gardner of Washington focuses on what he calls the "political alchemy" he practiced in making some significant educational reforms without substantial new resources. Governor Dick Thornburgh of Pennsylvania chronicles the first five days and aftermath of the Three Mile Island nuclear accident, which he describes as "an emergency management situation no governor has faced before or since." Governor Terry Branstad of Iowa describes the process, results, and lessons learned from restructuring and downsizing Iowa state government, a task he then considered his "proudest accomplishment." Governor Richard Lamm of Colorado details a somewhat different approach of selective review and improvement of the management and efficiency of state government agencies and functions. Governor John Sununu of New Hampshire illustrates a number of his philosophies of governing, both administratively and programmatically.

Each of the essays provides a "governor's-eye" view of governing. All offer insight into the vision, skills, and approaches governors use to get results—the "bottom line" of governing.

Governor Charles S. Robb
★ Virginia ★

Governor Robb currently serves as a Democratic U.S. senator for Virginia. He was governor of Virginia from 1982 to 1986, during which time he was chairman of the NGA Committee on Criminal Justice and Public Protection. He also served on the NGA Executive Committee.

After graduating from the University of Wisconsin and the University of Virginia Law School, Governor Robb served on active duty with the U.S. Marine Corps, including combat service in Vietnam. Following his military service, he practiced law in Richmond, Virginia, and Washington, D.C., and then served as lieutenant governor of Virginia.

His remarks as a gubernatorial fellow were made at Duke University on March 28, 1985.

increasing state needs, Delaware Governor Michael Castle describes how he turned the tables—through economic development and management improvements—to substantially increase state revenues, decrease state tax burdens, and improve the efficiency and effectiveness of state services. He details the key elements of his approach.

Utah Governor Scott Matheson places the issues of funding and delivery of services in a much broader intergovernmental perspective. He provides a historical account of the changing roles of the federal, state, and local governments, noting and illustrating the dramatic diffusion of power from the federal government to the state governments in recent decades. With that power and pivotal role for the states come increasing challenges for the nation's governors.

South Carolina Governor Richard Riley looks within the state at the balance of powers between the legislative and executive branches. Tracing historical changes in gubernatorial powers, yet citing continuing limits within his own state, he identifies and illustrates several ways that governors can get results, regardless of the formal institutional powers they are accorded.

From these historical and contemporary perspectives, several themes emerge that provide current and future contexts for governing. The states and the governors are becoming more and more powerful, intergovernmentally and institutionally. With seemingly unlimited expectations and increasingly limited resources, the governors cannot rely on those powers alone to "deliver" results. Enlightened leadership and management are the keys to gubernatorial success.

★ ★ ★ ★ ★

Overview

The citizens of a state expect much from their governor. They demand results, yet economic conditions, constitutional limits, and the intergovernmental system often constrain the governor's resources and powers to produce those results. The ultimate challenge of being a governor is to discover, among competing and often conflicting demands for service and within constrained resources and powers, the opportunity for state government to deliver those public services that the citizens most want and need.

The states share governing responsibilities with their federal and local partners, each of those governmental "players" having distinctive roles to play and resources to allocate. All states are affected by the national economy, with many experiencing significant swings in federal and state financial resources and in the demand for services. Each state endows its governor with institutional powers to govern, varying considerably from state to state. These roles and resources and powers provide the essential contexts for governing. In this beginning part, four governors describe one or more of these contexts and illustrate how constraints can be converted to opportunities and results.

Virginia Governor Charles Robb focuses on the allocation of resources. In what he terms "the Age of Limits," he points to the clear and urgent imperative for careful fiscal management. He outlines three components of the approach he followed: a fiscal policy that stressed level funding of existing programs, a thorough assessment of all programs, and a reorganization to streamline bureaucracy—all to help free state resources for new and compelling state needs.

Faced with the similar prospect of declining federal funds and ever-

★ ★ ★ ★ ★

PART ONE
CONTEXTS FOR GOVERNING

★ ★ ★ ★ ★

The Age of Limits:
Its Challenges and Opportunities

As governor of the state of Virginia, I have been fortunate to occupy a unique vantage point from which to observe the extent to which our society is continually changing. The expectations of our people and the ability of our government to meet them are undergoing a transformation — and in a fundamental way. The task before us is to hold to the best traditions of the past as we develop new ways of coping with the challenges that all of us know the future will bring. How well we respond to them will determine our chances of success. Our immediate task is establishing a solid foundation for the reorientation of governmental management that will be required during the remainder of the century.

We live in the Age of Limits — an era in which we have become keenly aware of our limits as a nation and of the restrictions on our ability to satisfy the demands of all the interest groups that have a voice in state and national affairs. Because the resources available to government with which to serve its people are restricted, it is the responsibility of elected officials to evaluate critically the services that are provided. We must continue to do what is essential, discontinue what is nonessential, and assume responsibility for those new services that the changing times will ultimately demand.

Our democratic traditions have by their very success raised the expectations of the citizenry to the point where there is a risk of crippling our form of government. Constituency groups throughout the country have learned to seek satisfaction for their own needs without regard to whether or not the states or the nation can afford to meet them. The enormous growth of state and local government has been driven by the desire to satisfy the diverse needs of our society without sufficient attention to costs.

The imperatives that point to careful fiscal management are therefore clear and urgent. To fail to act would constitute a real abdication of the responsibilities of democratic governance. In Virginia, during my term as governor, awareness of these limitations on growth led us to reevaluate carefully the role of state government in the lives of the people and the services we provide them. This process had three components, all of which were vital to its success.

First, a fiscal policy that stressed level funding of existing programs — a necessary step to make it possible to reshape state government without a tax increase. Second, a thorough assessment of all programs, and their elimination if they did not prove to be essential. Finally, a reorganization in order to streamline bureaucracy, to combine duplicative services, to reduce the burden of regulation, and to enable us simply to do more with less.

One of the most important results of this realignment was to free up additional funding for education, an area in which the need was critical. We funded state pay increases for our teachers amounting to 40 percent over a three-and-one-half-year period. We pumped more than a billion dollars beyond regular appropriations into all levels of education. In fact, spending in this field increased from 51 percent to 57 percent of our general fund budget. These monies have generated programs that will help prepare our people for the high-tech, fast-changing age that is upon us.

Perhaps the most exciting of the new programs is our Center for Innovative Technology, a research center in the northern part of the state for which the Virginia General Assembly appropriated more than $30 million in 1984. Functioning as a bridge between high-tech industries in the state and its institutions of higher learning, the center will use state-of-the-art technology to bring together business leaders seeking the latest research and scientists looking for practical applications of their studies. This sort of cooperation is almost impossible now, given the rapidly changing nature of the whole spectrum of high-tech research and development.

Additionally, programs such as our Televised Graduate Engineering Instruction effort, designed to allow engineers in the field to benefit from the latest research at our engineering schools, and the Continuous Electron Beam Accelerator Facility, which will spur research in high-energy-particle physics, will help Virginia as well as the entire Southeast enter the brave new high-tech world of tomorrow.

Even as we funded these new programs, we made huge strides in our reorganization of state government. First, through the concept of level funding, we budgeted 76 out of 102 state agencies and institutions for each year of the 1984-86 biennium at or below their funding levels for 1983. Twenty-one of those 76 agencies received additional funds targeted at new or expanded missions, such as promoting economic development, cleaning up the Chesapeake Bay, or meeting essential human needs. At the same time, we eliminated a number of unneeded services and achieved a more balanced staffing pattern. Since the reorganization was begun in 1982, we have increased worker productivity and reduced the employment level by 3,500 employees, without losing essential services. Additionally, we have reviewed more than 40,000 state rules and regulations and proposed that more than 40 percent of them either be eliminated or modified substantially. And more than a dozen state agencies have been abolished or combined with others at considerable savings to the taxpayer.

As the nation struggles to comprehend the uncomfortable idea that its resources are not limitless, those who serve in government must cope with the traditional interplay among interest groups that has forced the growth of state government in the past and that still places almost irresistible pressure on the federal government as it seeks to live within its means.

What goes by the name of "government" encompasses a range of human activity as diverse in nature and social value as the citizenry it serves. I believe that what distinguishes one government from another is the goals that it sets. And the character of any government is the aggregate of the aspirations and principles of all the people who comprise it.

That the populace does not necessarily discern the differences among agencies and sees only "government" is the government's fault. Why? It is in the nature of those who lead to talk only to their colleagues and to bask in the approval of those who already agree with them. Government should not complain of being misunderstood as long as its practitioners are unwilling, at the risk of being wrong, to test their ideas and beliefs against those of others in that strenuous contest of values by which the people set their goals, establish their priorities, and make up their minds on issues of public policy.

It is the lack of interchange that causes citizens, even the most sophisticated and knowledgeable of them, to remain in large measure ignorant about the nature of management's task in government. I believe that the basic job of government today is a never-ending effort to balance the overlapping and frequently competing agendas of special interest groups. In attempting to balance these diverse demands—in striving to meet too many demands with too few resources—all public managers can be certain of is that if they develop programs to serve everyone, no one will be perfectly satisfied with them.

While our citizens are preoccupied with that faceless abstraction called "government," we risk forgetting that what goes by that name is an intensely human activity. I cannot claim that people who work in government are any better than the populace at large; I am sure they are as good. The strength of government ultimately resides in the people.

The drive to satisfy the diverse goals of all segments of society has given rise to enormous growth in the public sector. If this trend is not somehow reversed, we are in danger of creating a destructive imbalance between the public and private sectors. We must depend on both of them together to accomplish our economic and social goals. We must plan more effectively as a nation for a more responsible allocation of those limited resources that we do have. This very difficult task of learning to say "no" cannot be successfully fulfilled without adhering to two age-old truths: There is no freedom without liability and there is no opportunity without cost.

We must restore balance to our society and our government if we are to endure and thrive in the Age of Limits. I do not believe, however, that this is a prescription for timidity or inaction. Only bold new programs that effectively confront the new realities will bring the United States into the twenty-first century prosperous and free and proud of its role as the world's innovator.

Thomas Henry Huxley, the English scientist, once wrote:

> There is a well-known adage that those who set out upon a great enterprise will do well to count the cost. I'm not sure that this is always entirely true. I think some of the very greatest enterprises in this world have been carried out simply because the people who undertook them did not count the costs. I am much of the opinion that often the more instructive considera-tion for us is the cost of doing nothing.

The cost of doing nothing in the Age of Limits is losing our place among the nations as a bastion of democracy and our spirit of enterprise.

Governor Michael N. Castle
★ Delaware ★

Governor Castle has served as the Republican governor of Delaware since 1985. He is a member of the NGA Executive Committee. He also has chaired the NGA Committee on Justice and Public Safety and has served as a lead governor on welfare reform for NGA.

The governor has been involved in state government throughout his career. After earning a bachelor's degree from Hamilton College and a law degree from Georgetown University, he served as state deputy attorney general. He then spent ten years in the Delaware General Assembly, two years as a representative and eight years as a state senator. Governor Castle also was lieutenant governor of Delaware.

His remarks as a gubernatorial fellow were made at Duke University on October 21, 1987.

★ ★ ★ ★ ★

Overcoming Fiscal Constraints: The Roles of Economic Development and Management Improvement

As chief executive officers of our respective states, we governors face the crucial task of matching available resources to the needs of our citizens. In the last few years, those needs have increased and the problems have become more complex. At the same time, our long-time partner and the source of much of the funding for many of these services, the federal government, is reducing its contributions.

In Delaware, we have responded in two ways. First, we have intensified our economic development efforts, with one of our goals being an increase in state revenues. Second, we have very aggressively attempted to improve our management practices.

The results have been gratifying. State revenues have increased substantially. We have increased the quantity and enhanced the quality of our services. We are rendering these services more efficiently. In fact, we have done so well on each of these fronts that we have also been able to halve our citizens' income tax burden.

I am proud of what we have done and of the innovative and dedicated people who made our successes possible. To Illustrate, I will describe both the philosophy that has guided us and some of our more important initiatives.

Economic Development

First, we believe that economic growth is the key to the quality of life in our state. A strong economy provides opportunities for each of us to achieve personal growth and economic independence, and for the state to address legitimate needs for service.

Therefore, we have been committed to expanding our economic base by diversifying our economy and capitalizing on Delaware's unique assets. We are constantly seeking incentives that attract new businesses to Delaware and to support the expansion of businesses already located here.

Our state economy does not stand alone. Competition for new and expanded business and for employable workers is heavy within our Middle Atlantic region. Accordingly, we are constantly monitoring regional economic trends. As quickly as we can, we attempt to implement measures that keep Delaware an attractive place to do business.

We are especially interested in developing business that matches the skills of our labor market, complements our natural environment, and contributes to our economic security.

Our Financial Center Development Act (FCDA) is an example. Under it, we liberalized our consumer credit regulations and, in a variety of ways, made it attractive to banks to relocate their operations to Delaware. A large number of banks responded by moving their credit card operations to our state. We had a good supply of well-qualified clerical personnel and managers, our housing costs and general quality of life were attractive to many who faced relocating, and our local legal community and courts offered a level of sophistication equal to or better than the level that the banks had experienced elsewhere.

The result: more than 6,000 new jobs have been created during the last five years in the banking industry alone.

Although FCDA is the outstanding example, our pro-business philosophy has brought dramatic growth in many other areas of our economy. During a period when many states experienced a recession, we both lowered our unemployment rate to well below the national average and experienced significant in-migration of jobs.

To maintain this momentum, our Department of Finance regularly reviews our tax system with the goal of improving our regional competitiveness and correcting inequities that might discourage business from locating in Delaware.

We also place great emphasis on the development and maintenance of a skilled workforce. It is, if you will, our human capital. This policy requires a concerted effort on the part of our elementary, secondary, and adult education systems and of our job training programs.

Our Department of Labor and our Development Office constantly monitor the kinds and levels of skills needed by our businesses. In this most recent fiscal year, we placed our greatest emphasis on entry-level skills. Our Department of Labor takes the lead in encouraging this training, but its actual delivery involves both the public and private sectors.

This constant monitoring has paid other dividends. First, the labor department's ongoing compilation of data has allowed us to be assured that current and proposed training is aimed at actual labor market needs.

Second, our Department of Health and Social Services has been able to use this data to design programs under our "First Step" welfare reform program to give to welfare recipients the training and guidance that have enabled them to obtain jobs and to get off our welfare rolls.

We also see public education as crucial to the development of an excellent workforce. From the outset of the administration, we have been seeking significant improvement in our schools. Much of the groundwork was laid in 1983-84 by our Governor's Task Force on Education for Economic Growth. It highlighted the crucial contribution public education could make to sustaining economic growth and opportunity.

As a result, we are pursuing a number of school improvement initiatives at both the state and local levels. We have given highest priority to the following initiatives:

• Development of curriculum content standards for all basic skills courses, kindergarten through twelfth grade.

• Development of a testing system to monitor progress in these areas and to identify areas where remediation is required.

• A significant increase in teacher salaries and professional development programs.

Because we anticipate an increasing demand for workers to move from job to job and to take on responsibilities previously given to middle managers, we want our schools to intensify their efforts to develop students' capacities for critical thinking, communication, and problem solving.

It has become increasingly clear that all of today's students will have to be productive workers in the years ahead. We cannot lose them to dropping out. Therefore, we have found an increasing number of ways to encourage local school districts to emphasize attendance, positive work habits, and alternative education programs.

Because we know that we can identify many of those at risk of dropping out in the elementary grades, we are beginning to emphasize early interventions. To provide a coherent and research-based approach, I will soon commission a high-level task force of experts and both public and private representatives to design and implement a comprehensive multiyear strategy for reducing the dropout rate.

We also know that when children receive proper school readiness training at home, in preschool, or in day care, their chances for success in school are vastly improved. Therefore, we are piloting a Four-Year-Old Development Program, and we have formed an Early Childhood Education Study Committee to provide recommendations for the strengthening of our preschool readiness opportunities.

A policy of ongoing investment and maintenance in infrastructure is fundamental to sustained economic development and our ability to deliver essential services. One widely quoted study has estimated that unless there is an intensified commitment to public reinvestment, as much as 75 percent of the nation's communities will be unable to participate in economic development programs. In the mid-1970s many states chose to defer essential infrastructure maintenance, a policy decision reflected today in overcrowded state facilities, congested highways, and overburdened wastewater treatment systems.

We have concluded that if Delaware is to continue to build on its recent economic successes, we must take carefully measured steps to ensure that our infrastructure can support the future demands that will be placed upon it. We believe it is critical that we maintain our capital investments and carefully target our available resources.

Accordingly, we have revised our capital budgeting process, accelerated our drive to bring all state facilities up to accepted standards, and dedicated certain revenue to capital projects through an initiative called the First State Improvement Fund.

Because deferred maintenance and capital investment are frequently ignored by governments, we believed that we needed to improve the level of public understanding and acceptance of these activities and to cultivate the support of opinion leaders. To do this, we instituted public hearings for all departments' capital requests, required them to submit three-year capital plans, and created a ranking system that effectively set a single set of priorities statewide. Finally, we implemented a plan to improve identification of departmental space needs, to encourage disposal of state surplus property, and to intensify use of state facilities.

Management Improvements

State government in Delaware is a big business. If the state of Delaware was ranked on the Fortune 500 list, we would be number 253. Like all other well-run businesses, the state must constantly evaluate its performance and look for more efficient ways to provide services.

To pursue these goals in a methodical way, we established four objectives, each of which we have pursued from the beginning of our tenure.

Our first objective is to improve customer service.

We see ourselves as being in the "service sector." Therefore, we must continually work to improve the quality, reliability, and satisfaction these services provide. We must take pride in our "products" and listen to our customers.

By way of example, we recently supported a Public Satisfaction Study. This project surveyed public perceptions on topics such as the quality of the information provided by our service centers and the degree to which services were delivered in a timely and professional manner.

This study provided participating agencies with the necessary data to identify deficiencies and gaps in service. Agencies have been modifying their delivery systems in accord with the findings. Happily, most of the suggested changes have been minor and easily implemented.

Our second objective is to be forward-looking.

Our environment and the needs of our citizens are in a state of constant change. The adoption of the shortsighted quick fix or "we have always done it this way" approach often dooms initiatives to failure. We press our agencies to make every effort to anticipate emerging needs and to develop policies that address issues in a preventive fashion. To achieve this objective, we have begun to have our departments articulate multiyear program goals and initiatives.

To enhance our performance in this area we have expanded the use of the state's econometric model. We believe this model makes particular sense for agencies like our Departments of Labor, Transportation, and Health and Social Services, which necessarily must rely on relatively long-term predictions in their planning.

Another example is our Delaware Environmental Legacy Program. Through a public-private task force we are attempting to focus attention on the difficult decisions we face in attempting to balance continued development against the protection of our environment.

We have directed our departments to give priority to active participation in this process and to implementation of the group's recommendations.

Our third objective is to work smarter.

Too often government and other large organizations stifle innovation because they are unwilling to change long-standing operating procedures and policies. As federal funding and growth in resources decline, failed and outdated solutions and "throwing more money at the problem" are not options for government to exercise. We have tried to do more with less resources and to develop more creative and cost-efficient methods of resource management.

Last year, we implemented a budget process requiring departments to divorce their planning processes from their budget requests, to adopt multiyear goals and objectives, and to base their plans on a methodical review of both what they were currently doing and what major issues they expected to face in the future. As a result, agencies have become increasingly conscious of the need to identify issues before they impact our resources; they are increasingly willing to consider the reallocation of existing resources as well as the termination of unsuccessful programs; and we are allocating our resources in ways more consistent with our long-term goals.

We also have been moving toward increased reliance on computer-based technology. We already have begun to see improvements in data gathering and analysis, in reduced manpower requirements for recordkeeping and other clerical responsibilities, and in faster processing times for numerous documents.

Our fourth objective is to promote cooperation and collaboration among departments.

Crucial to meeting the twin challenges of increasing needs and diminishing resources is the coordination of resources and services across public agency lines and between the public and private sectors.

Early in our administration, we established four interagency "cabinet councils" and the Office of State Planning and Coordination. The councils were charged with identifying emerging issues that cut across agency responsibilities, developing plans to address interagency concerns, and improving the coordination of service delivery. The planning office has provided staff support to the councils and directly manages selected interagency projects.

To develop and sustain this commitment to a team approach to the productivity improvements we have expected, we have conscientiously sought ways to encourage and reward demonstrations of these values.

To those ends, we strongly supported the work and the recommendations of our State Compensation and Productivity Commission. The commission recommended steps to align pay more closely with performance and productivity and proposed significant revisions in both our evaluation system and our pay scales. We followed through, implementing both sets of recommendations.

The commission also recommended, and we have created, a Management Fellows Program and a Management Development Institute. Together, these programs are designed to develop Delaware-specific adaptations of promising management initiatives, to encourage and cultivate innovative and productive efforts by our employees, and to identify and develop those employees with demonstrated managerial potential.

Conclusion

This compilation is of course neither an exhaustive list of our efforts in these two critical areas nor a complete catalog of good practice. It does, however, suggest an approach that we have found fruitful. We start with a philosophy that recognizes our state's economy as the engine that drives our ability to provide services. It follows that we in government should encourage business growth and we should emphasize the creation and maintenance of a citizenry ready, willing, and able to work diligently and skillfully. We must provide the wherewithall to accomplish both goals.

We see a similar obligation to manage well and efficiently. We constantly look for ways to improve customer service, to work smarter, to be forward-looking, and to promote collaboration and cooperation among our employees and our agencies.

By doing all these things, we have increased the resources available to meet our citizens' needs, reduced their income tax burden, increased and enhanced our services, and improved our efficiency.

Governor Scott M. Matheson
★ Utah ★

Governor Matheson is a lawyer with the firm of Parsons, Behle, and Latimer in Salt Lake City, Utah. He was the Democratic governor of Utah from 1977 to 1985. Governor Matheson served as chairman of NGA in 1982-83, was chairman of the first NGA Subcommittee on Water Management, and was the lead governor on the federal budget.

Prior to his election as governor in 1976, Governor Matheson was general solicitor for the Union Pacific Railroad Company. His law career has included the positions of assistant general counsel for Anaconda Company, deputy Salt Lake County attorney, and Parowan city attorney. Governor Matheson graduated from the University of Utah and Stanford Law School.

His remarks as a gubernatorial fellow were made at Duke University on November 7, 1984.

★ ★ ★ ★ ★

Intergovernmental Relations
and the New Federalism

Intergovernmental relations and the New Federalism are of tremendous importance to states, local governments, and those who make policy decisions at the federal level. These two concepts deal with how a federal governmental system that is made up of several integral parts operates effectively—specifically, how the federal, state, and local governmental processes function and interrelate within the rules of the Constitution. During the 1980s, some major changes took place in this area.

This is mainly because President Ronald Reagan's victories in 1980 and 1984 gave him a mandate—expecially concerning his personal philosophy about intergovernmental relationships. Based on this philosophy, he created the New Federalism,[1] which notably enhanced the role of the states. This development has attracted the strong interest not only of politicians and public administrators but also of political scientists, historians, and other scholars as well as public policy specialists.

In my opinion, President Reagan has shown more interest in the "proper" role of the state and federal governments than any president since Woodrow Wilson. He really does have a personal commitment to reduce the role of the federal government—whether one agrees with him or not on how to bring that about. He has also had the unique opportunity to be on the other side of the fence—as governor for eight years of most populous state in the nation. So he brought the discipline of a state chief executive and added to it eight years of presidential experience, during which he was personally committed to reducing the role of the federal government.

The major question most governors, mayors, county commissioners, and state legislators are asking is whether the president's New Federalism is merely a smoke screen to transfer the costs to the states of programs that have been created at the federal level by the Congress or whether it involves trying to decide which level of government can best carry out essential public services. Another reason why the New Federalism is critical today is the huge federal budget deficit, which keeps mounting regardless of the healthy economy.

Despite Walter Mondale's persistent attempt to make that deficit an issue in the 1984 campaign, he did not stir the imagination of the voters on the issue. They do not understand it as thoroughly as perhaps they might, and frankly they are probably not interested in it because it has not seriously affected them personally. But you cannot continue to borrow more money each year than taxes bring in. Then a permanent mismatch of revenues and expenditures exists. The federal deficit creates high interest rates, which ultimately slow the economy and bring about serious recessionary periods. Interest-sensitive industries that have been the hardest hit are agricultural exports, housing, and capital expansion—all important to governors as they try to keep their states afloat.

The proper role of the federal and state governments has been a subject of debate throughout the nation's history. Madison asserted in *The Federalist* *(Number 14)* that if the states were abolished, "the general government would be compelled by the principle of self-preservation to reinstate them in their proper jurisdiction." Political leaders ranging from Adlai Stevenson to Louis Brandeis to Oliver Wendell Holmes stress in all their writings that the states are the laboratories of democracy: the insulated chambers for experimentation in policy and in law. Stevenson regarded the power of the states to decide legitimate local affairs as one of the great assets of our free society, making possible democratic participation at the grass roots of human relations.

In modern times, the states are operating efficiently and are no longer cumbersome and outmoded institutions. They have also learned how to be responsive to local concerns. In recent decades, a dramatic diffusion of power from the federal to the state governments has occurred. Yet, the founders of our nation perceived that state sovereignty if unchecked could even endanger the survival of the nation. Hamilton, the centralist, in *The Federalist (Number 17)*, contended that "it would always be far more easy for the state governments to encroach upon the national authorities than for the national government to encroach upon the state authorities." He concluded that great care needed to be exercised to give the central government all the force compatible with the principles of liberty.

At the federal level, interpretations of the commerce and the general health and welfare clauses of the Constitution and the Fourteenth Amendment have had a major impact. Woodrow Wilson claimed way back in 1911 that the "proper balance of the state and national power cannot be settled at all by the opinion of one generation." In other words, the metamorphosis must be very slow and the experimentation lengthy and careful. And so the roles are evolving constantly. Hamilton's comments may be a little inapplicable today because there is little fear of state encroachment on federal authority. Also, an examination of the nature of Supreme Court operation during the last three decades reveals that most of what Hamilton was concerned about has now been articulated and ratified.

During Franklin D. Roosevelt's New Deal, beginning in 1933, federal power was greatly augmented. The centralization in grant programs changed the nature of the intergovernmental system. But in the entire 1930-1970 period, only 132 grant-in-aid programs were enacted, primarily for highways, old-age assistance, aid to dependent children, and employment security. No one in all those years even debated the question of whether or not the federal government was taking over state functions.

In the 1960s, the states defaulted their responsibility in the intergovernmental system. They did not even compete for their proper role in what should properly be administered on their level. Therefore, the grant-in-aid system skyrocketed. That was the period when the states refused to consider the needs of local units of government. The mayors and county commissioners were dying on the vine, possessing no taxing authority except what the legislatures begrudgingly gave them. Suddenly, mayors and county commissioners were flying to Washington, D.C., and telling Congress: "Those governors out there are ignoring us, those legislators are not willing to look at our problem, help us." And Congress did.

In the 1960s, other dramatic changes occurred in the nation's intergovernmental system. The judiciary alone had a dramatic impact: the extension of the Fourteenth Amendment, the desegregation cases, the criminal due process rulings, the legislative reapportionment, and the voting rights cases. During that same decade, major Great Society initiatives were made by President Johnson, and medical care was greatly expanded.

During the 1970s, some minor intergovernmental reform initiatives were made, but they only increased the complexity. That was the period when revenue-sharing started, in the Nixon administration. President Jimmy Carter reduced the program, and today it no longer exists at the state level, though local units of government still benefit from it.

After the Vietnam and Watergate experiences, citizens viewed the "imperial presidency" somewhat like President Roosevelt was regarded when he tried to pack the Supreme Court back in the 1930s. The time was ripe for a president to come along and transfer some of the power and funds back to the lower units of government. That is exactly what Ronald Reagan did when he became president in 1980.

By that time, grants-in-aid to state and local governments totaled $91.5 billion—a doubling of funds between 1968 and 1980. For example, 209 new grant-in-aid programs were enacted during Johnson's Great Society era of the 1960s, 90 during the Nixon-Ford period, and 70 during the Carter era. By the end of 1980, some 540 categorical federal grant programs were on the books—an explosion. By that year, the predominant federal-state partnership of 1960 had become one where every state, every county, all cities and towns, nearly all school districts, at least half of the nation's special districts along with twenty multistate economic development groups, 1,500 sub-state regional units, hundreds of nonprofit organizations, and dozens of colleges and universities were all receiving direct federal aid.

When I was elected as governor of Utah, I had absolutely no idea about the importance of that office and intergovernmental relationships, particularly with respect to the federal system. When two senators and a number of congressmen are representing state interests, what actions are required of governors to protect their states when their main functions are to serve at the state capitol, manage the executive branch, and work with the state legislature?

However, governors cannot really appreciate the impact of the federal government throughout their states until they assume office and see exactly how the intergovernmental system operates. Recognizing this, I instinctively responded and opened up an office for Utah in Washington, D.C., to increase its involvement in managing federal programs and lands. Nearly 70 percent of the land in Utah is owned by the federal government; the secretary of the interior is a bigger landlord than the governor. The state's economy and future, which are closely tied into those federal lands, depend to a great extent on creating positive relationships with the secretary of the interior.

Governors finally have learned that if they do not spend a major portion of their time outside their states, especially in Washington, they deprive their citizens of an opportunity to receive their fair share of federal resources, and federal policy will change the nature of state policymaking and expenditures. Because most senators and members of Congress lack sufficient knowledge about the activities of the executive branch of the federal government in Washington, they cannot be relied on to protect the states' interests. This can be achieved only by the governors, other state representatives, and the executive branch.

In 1959 Congress established the Advisory Commission on Intergovernmental Relations, consisting of about twenty-six governors, senators, and mayors. The commission determined that the biggest problem in intergovernmental relations was the increasingly intrusive, unmanageable, ineffective, and costly role of the federal government in nearly every aspect of people's daily lives.

The federal share of the gross national product (GNP) grew from 2 percent in 1929 to 23 percent in 1980, the year Reagan was elected, even though not all the federal bills were being paid. During the same period, the combined share of the GNP for all other units of government—the states and counties and cities—increased at a much less dramatic rate (that is, from 5 percent to 11 percent). This is an unbelievable rise in revenue at the federal level, though some of it came about for legitimate reasons. Reacting to these factors—as well as the war in Vietnam, Watergate, the war on poverty, stagflation, and interest rates—Reagan also discovered that governors, legislators, and mayors were anxious to participate more fully in intergovernmental operations. They wanted to be full partners and help make the policy as well as decide on how the money would be spent so that constituents would receive a fair share of the distribution.

Many of the governors were also dissatisfied with the role of Congress. George Busbee, governor of Georgia, who was chairman of the National Governors' Association, said, "Pothole repair, fire fighting, garbage disposal, building codes, jellyfish control are all subjects of solemn deliberations on the Potomac. *The Congressional Record* sometimes bears an uncanny resemblance to the minutes of a county commission meeting." George was right. The Congress of the United States is too concerned about matters involving county commissioners and mayors and spends too much time worrying about what the states properly and adequately can do. The role of individual members of Congress has also been affected by the newly emerged Frostbelt-Sunbelt issue.

Indicative of the new trend is the national emergence of the state organizations. The National Governors' Association has assumed an aggressive stance on the Washington scene during the last ten years in an amazing metamorphosis. The governors used to get together twice a year, play golf, cruise from New York to the Bahamas, and that sort of thing. Today, they are so occupied with official business at their meetings and workshops that almost no time remains for the traditional social activities. The legislators, mayors, and county commissioners are similarly busy. National organizations representing these groups are growing larger and stronger every year.

John Naisbitt's book *Megatrends* points out that the trend in the United States is toward decentralization. Regardless of the desires of governmental officials, he contends, the public favors this approach; they want government closer and more responsive to them and their needs. Naisbitt also believes a present megatrend is a shift from a national economy to an international economy, a trend that is strongly affecting the economies of the states.

In his first inaugural address, President Reagan said, "It is my intention to curb the size and influence of the federal establishment and to demand recognition of the distinction between the powers granted to the federal government and those reserved to the states or to the people." He also presented some guiding principles. First, substitute state and local governments for the federal government in dealing with private institutions that receive federal aid. In other words, if federal money is granted to arts groups, why not let the state rather than someone in Washington manage it? Second, where appropriate, cap open-ended federal matching programs. Third, use block grants to combine and move categorical federal programs to the state and local levels. These are the basic mechanisms that have facilitated intergovernmental transfers. Another is to utilize the planning audit and review function at the state and local levels, but this has presented problems. The accountability to the federal government is so complex in many sets of circumstances that the money is hardly worth taking.

To alleviate this problem, an interesting proposal has been made to replace federal funding and move the revenue sources from federal to state and local governments: instead of the federal government receiving the tax and passing the bill, send the revenue directly to state general funds. Senator Dave Durenberger of Minnesota is a prominent advocate of devolution of funds and programs to the states. He believes that 10 percent of income-tax revenue should be given to the states. The idea behind these proposals is to locate the funding mechanism at the level where a service is performed.

Another idea that has been advanced is having state government rather than federal government deal with local government, when appropriate. Instead of mayors flying to Washington to confer with members of Congress and federal administrators, why not have them consult their governors? Some governors still do not like to see mayors or county commissioners, I am sorry to say. But I do because that is the way to obtain intergovernmental cooperation.

In response to President Reagan's proposals on intergovernmental transfers, in 1981 the governors suggested block grants, the combining of a group of categorical grants into a package that allows flexibility in the way the funds are spent. In other words, if funds are not needed in one category, they can be applied to another category in the block grant. Because of the efficiency provided by this flexibility, a 10 percent cut in the total would be possible. Congress offered a 25 percent cut and no flexibility, but later increased the flexibility somewhat, and nine major block grants were created that year. They have been used since that time with some degree of success.

In 1982 President Reagan proposed that Medicaid be completely federalized despite the skyrocketing costs if the states would manage the Aid to Families with Dependent Children (AFDC) and Food Stamp programs as well as about forty-three categoricals. To pay for those programs, the federal government would establish a trust fund. The governors, however, were opposed to assuming responsibility for both funding and managing income security programs such as AFDC and Food Stamps.

Therefore, the governors suggested that these two programs be set aside and that federalizing Medicaid be discussed. The governors proposed that the states take the $10 billion that they contributed and in return they would operate a group of categoricals at the state level. To further the negotiations, the famous "Swap Team" was organized, consisting of six governors, including myself, Dick Snelling of Vermont, George Busbee of

Georgia, Bruce Babbitt of Arizona, Lamar Alexander of Tennessee, and Jim Thompson of Illinois. The president appointed Ed Meese, Jim Baker, David Stockman, and Rich Williamson[2] to sit down with the team and negotiate how to handle the income security issues. The governors wanted the federal government to handle them, and they were willing to take the savings and an equal amount of categoricals. Despite a series of meetings at the White House during the spring and summer, the negotiations were unsuccessful.

About that time, the 1982 election occurred right in the middle of a serious recession. Suddenly, intergovernmental relations and federalism were very unpopular because all the governors and locally elected people perceived that the problems of the federal government were being shifted to the states by cutting the amount of the money they were receiving—and they had already taken a 20 percent cut. Because the domestic portion of the federal budget is less than 15 percent of the total, the budget cannot be balanced even if all the funds are denied to the states. In view of the recession and the budget problem, all the attention shifted quickly away from federalism and a period of budget debate began.

In that regard, at a governors' meeting with David Stockman, he stated that though the administration and the governors favored federalism, he did not believe that issue was relevant to that of the budget. I responded, "Mr. Stockman, they have relevancy—they *are* one and the other."

The philosophical problems about the efficient management of the intergovernmental system are just as complex today as they were during the 1981-82 dialogue with the president and his staff. As Woodrow Wilson said, "A whole generation is not enough time to digest this very complex situation." Yet some progress had been made that cannot be retracted. Public policy is just not changed at the federal level without meeting the needs of those who are legitimately impacted by it.

In retrospect, the governors made a serious mistake in 1981-82. As is often their fashion, perhaps intentionally, they ignored the legislators, who are also policymakers. Without consulting Congress, how could a practical, achievable, efficient intergovernmental relationship be created? On the other side of the coin, senators and members of Congress are not likely to favor devolving power away from themselves. It is difficult for senators who have been back in the Senate for three or four terms to vote to give away power that they helped create in categorical bills fifteen years earlier. In addition, the constituencies who are the beneficiaries of those categoricals do not want to see them changed. Also, the federal employees who administer the programs obviously take a similar stance.

Ever since *Baker v. Carr*,[3] state governments have strengthened themselves dramatically. They are not amateur players in the intergovernmental framework; they are sophisticated and modern governmental operations. They are prepared to meet the challenges that lie ahead in the continually changing federal and intergovernmental systems.

Governor Richard W. Riley
★ South Carolina ★

Governor Riley is currently an attorney with the law firm of Nelson, Mullins, Riley, and Scarborough in Columbia, South Carolina. He served as the Democratic governor of South Carolina from 1979 to 1987. He was a member of the NGA Executive Committee and chairman of the NGA Education Task Force on Readiness.

Governor Riley graduated from Furman University and served two years in the Navy as a communications officer. Following his naval service, the governor earned a law degree from the South Carolina School of Law. He was then elected and served four years in the South Carolina House of Representatives, followed by service in the State Senate.

His remarks as a gubernatorial fellow were made at Duke University on September 10, 1986.

★ ★ ★ ★ ★

Overcoming Restrictions on Gubernatorial Authority: The Unique Problems of Some Governors

In a state where the constitution assigns strong powers to the legislature and restricts those of the governor, the incumbent faces special challenges and must utilize unique governance techniques. My state, South Carolina, is an example. Its form of government is typical of the kind that was organized in the thirteen original states more than two hundred years ago. Although these new state governments were based on the revolutionary principle of indirect democracy (or government by representation), they were also organized with an eye toward the recent experience with the British Crown.

The Founding Fathers not only were ardent followers of the English Enlightenment and the French philosophical movement, but also were eminently practical politicians. Following Locke's "social contract" thesis, they viewed government as a necessary instrument of social order, but one that had to be controlled so that it would not be used to abuse the citizens it was supposed to serve. Thus, the founders divided their state governments into three branches, which were characterized by the "separation of powers" and "checks and balances" safeguards. The three branches included a weak executive and a strong legislature. An excellent example of this is South Carolina, where the governor was selected by the General Assembly from 1776 up until 1865. (Under the Crown, the governor was appointed by the king, and the colonial assembly was selected by the people.)

Obviously, this form of government was satisfying to the eighteenth-century leadership in the newly formed states. So when the decision was made to send delegates to Philadelphia to design a new national government, the same principles were incorporated into the new federal Constitution.

This emphasis on legislative power lasted throughout the nineteenth century at both the state and the national levels. Despite an occasional strong president—like Jefferson, Jackson, and Lincoln—it was not until Theodore Roosevelt and Woodrow Wilson that the power and prestige of the modern presidency began to emerge.

At the state level, this shift in power was not initiated until the 1920s. Upon his election as governor of New York in 1918, Al Smith commissioned Robert Moses[4] to study the reorganization of state government. In his report, Moses concluded: "No citizen can hope to understand the present collection of departments, offices, boards, and commissions, or the present methods of appropriating money."

The solution proposed by Smith was a series of reforms to create a modern state government organized around a stronger governor. The principal features of this reform package were:

• A four-year term for the governor.

• Gubernatorial appointment of all state officials, except the governor, lieutenant governor, attorney general, and comptroller—in other words, cabinet government.

• An executive budget, prepared by the governor and submitted to the General Assembly.

Of course, the change in the balance of power between the legislative and the executive branches was quickly noted. To his critics, Governor-Elect Smith made this response: "The Governor does not hold office by hereditary right. He is elected for a fixed term by universal suffrage. He is controlled in all minor appointments by the civil service law. He cannot spend a dollar of the public money which is not authorized by the Legislature of the State."

During the 1920s and 1930s, the merits of Smith's form of state government were recognized and his reforms adopted—first in New York and then in many other states throughout the nation. But not in all of them. It was not until 1980 that South Carolina adopted just one of these reforms: the "two-term" amendment, the right of governors to succeed themselves in office. And Mississippi, another state where the executive was restricted, continued to adhere completely to the old system.

During the past two decades, a second wave of change has occurred in state government—a process that has been carefully documented by Professors Ann Bowman and Richard Kearney, of the University of South Carolina, in their book *The Resurgence of the States*. This resurgence has been enhanced by the New Federalism policies of Presidents Nixon, Ford, Carter, and Reagan.[5] It has been accompanied by the increasing professionalization of state legislatures. And it has been characterized by the reemergence of governors as stronger chief executives, as described by Professor Larry Sabato, of the University of Virginia, in his book *Goodbye to Good-Time Charlie: The American Governor Transformed.*

All these changes were noted by *Washington Post* columnist David S. Broder, who wrote from the National Governors' Association Annual

Meeting at Hilton Head in August 1986: "The most interesting and important dialogues in American government these days are those taking place at the governors' meetings. These folks . . . are seriously engaged with the issues of education, economic development, the environment, crime and drugs—issues which the voters understand will determine the future of this country."

Unlike the early twentieth-century reform movement toward modern state government—reforms that required legislative agreement to enact the proposed constitutional and statutory changes—this second wave was the result not of changes in the law, but of basic changes in the nature of the federal system and the role of government in our society and our economy—a transformation that was spurred by events and leaders and has taken place in all the fifty states, including mine.

Nevertheless, the power of the governors in a few states is still restricted. How do they govern when the rules of the game—both written and unwritten—give them relatively little formal authority? In South Carolina I found that a governor can influence the creation and furtherance of public policy in four ways, though these are some of the very tools upon which all governmental chief executives must rely, regardless of which level they occupy:

• Coordinating the system, including state agencies, boards, and commissions.

• Management and priority setting, primarily through the budget process.

• Influencing the legislature.

• Exerting leadership, which is possibly the most valuable power at the governor's disposal.

Of course, because of the enactment of the two-term amendment in South Carolina, these functions have assumed new and additional significance.

The first function is the coordination of the system through state agencies, boards, and commissions. The executive authority in the South Carolina state government rests chiefly with the boards, commissioners, and trustees who oversee the operation of the state agencies. This method of governance, however, results in a fragmented system. Yet the governors can overcome this diffusion of authority and help coordinate the system through their appointive powers to boards and commissions. However, these appointive powers may vary from agency to agency. For some state boards, the governor has complete appointive power; some require the consent of the state senate; and, in some, the board or commission members are elected directly by the legislature.

Because of the possibility of serving a second term, governors find their influence through appointments greatly enhanced. When they are first elected to office, they find that appointees from the previous incumbent hold most of the appointed positions under their discretion. It is not until the last two years of the first term that governors begin to see their own appointees exert influence on boards and commissions.

During the second term, however, most appointive positions have been filled with people the current governor has selected—appointees whom the governor hopes will reflect his or her executive style and priorities. In fact, as I neared the end of my tenure as the state's first two-term governor, I found that my appointees occupied virtually all the appointive positions open to me.

These appointments represent one of the few formal opportunities for governors to establish policies and procedures compatible with their own. Although I believe this avenue is a prime way for governors to exert their influence, it has always been my position that appointments should be made in a representative way and that a person's credentials should be carefully considered. Party affiliation or political background should not be the controlling factors. I have never thought that appointees should be clones of the governor. Rather, I sought thoughtful people who would give a good hearing to my ideas.

The second gubernatorial function is management through the budget process. It is often said that the budget is the most significant policy statement government makes, though this is often forgotten in the rush of numbers or the frenzy of the legislative session. Each state's budget says more about its priorities than any other single piece of legislation. However, the budget process, in and of itself, is not a policy tool. The leadership exerted concerning the budget is what sets priorities. And if that is effective, an executive can influence the budget, and through it, the policy of the state. Every election year in South Carolina, we hear much talk about the need for budget reform. However, regardless of the kind of process a state utilizes to achieve this goal, good budget management is dependent on strong leadership.

Although I lacked the power to sign an executive budget, I found that by emphasizing those issues I considered to be top priorities, I was able to use the system to advance them. This was done by corresponding annually early in the budget process with all state agencies and stressing my priorities. Then, as chairman of the State Budget and Control Board, I tried to reemphasize them when these same agency heads appeared at our annual budget hearings, held prior to the legislative session.

So I think it is more a question of leadership than of mechanics. The mechanics work well if the leadership is effective. A lot of time can be spent talking about the process—whether it is better for the budget to be initiated by the governor or the legislature. But in my judgment, what is really important is a viable product, which is best attained through hard work and the exercise of leadership.

The third function—a governor's relationship with the legislature—is a critical one. Effective performance in this role results in the enactment of laws that carry out gubernatorial policies and objectives. A key ingredient in the governor's relationship with the General Assembly is fairness, whether it is the governor's first or second term. This means the governor should be consistent and maintain unambiguous policies regarding vetoes. Remarks to the media should be clear and honest, and an open-door policy during sessions helps maintain rapport with the legislators, as does a hard-working and knowledgeable staff that will cooperate with them. All these factors are basic to successful dealings in a strong legislative state. However, the most critical one may be the final function I will address: the governors' leadership potential, which is their real source of power.

Just through the sheer force of leadership, governors can focus the attention of the people on an issue, explain what it is, and then move the state toward an equitable solution. To do this effectively, they must take time to understand their roles and how they personally will fit into the situation before deciding on a course of action. By setting the tone and coordinating the effort, they can crystallize the attention of the public on a problem and obtain their acceptance of a solution.

The best recent example of this process in my state was the reform of public education that began in 1983. By using the governor's office as a catalyst for change, we were able to spark a grass-roots reform effort that resulted not only in passage of nationally recognized education legislation, but also in a penny sales-tax increase that many political experts predicted we would never win.

Through the leadership potential inherent in the top statewide office, I took the case for quality education to the people. This was fertile ground because a statewide poll we had commissioned showed strong support for educational improvement, including a tax increase if it was needed. Armed with this information, we invited the public to attend one of seven forums around the state to express their views on improvement of our schools. The turnout was more than we ever imagined. Some 13,000 people attended the forums, which were actually "pep rallies" for better schools led by myself, the lieutenant governor, and the state superintendent of schools.

Concurrent with this grass-roots movement, I also used my office to assemble a blue-ribbon committee of the top business, educational, and legislative leadership in the state. Our school reform proposal was drafted by members of this committee, which was staffed by the education experts from my office. Once the proposal was completed, the full committee approved the report, called "A New Approach to Quality Education." Then, as a final public-rallying event, I went on statewide television—a method I had used only one other time during my tenure as governor.

About a month before the General Assembly convened, I made a televised address to explain the education proposal and to urge the passage of the penny sales-tax increase to fund it.

Thus, going into the session, we had very little opposition to the proposal itself, but found that opposition to the tax increase was still strong. It was on this point that the ability of the governor to focus statewide attention on an issue paid off. Because of the grass-roots support we had gathered, together with the influence of the business leaders we had won over to our cause, we were able to turn around the legislative opposition and win passage of what was to be called the Education Improvement Act of 1984 and the tax increase to fund it.

These events provide a good practical example of the influence even constitutionally "weak" executives can exert if their real source of power is tapped: the opportunity to lead. Many of the tools and devices available to a governor are subtle ones, both implied and assumed. Among them are the willingness to work; knowledge of the state and its governmental systems; the careful setting of goals; and, most of all, the capacity to lead. In the end, in carrying out all the functions of the governor, that is the critical ingredient.

The above four functions—coordination of the system, management and goal setting, influencing the legislature, and leadership—are the essential tools that must be employed by all governmental chief executives, whether the mayor of Anchorage or St. Louis or Miami, the governor of North Carolina or New York or South Carolina, or the president of the United States.

Why is the president in this list? After all, under the original U.S. Constitution, he had full appointive powers within the executive branch—in other words, he headed a cabinet government. Further, he served a four-year term with right of succession. And although the Constitution did not directly address the issue of the executive budget, he was one of the first governmental chief executives in this country to receive this authority, in the 1922 Budget and Accounting Act.

But I know that these tools are essential to the president because of a letter Harry Truman wrote to his sister almost forty years ago. Although it was at the height of what Arthur Schlesinger termed *The Imperial Presidency*, Truman complained to her that most people had a very inaccurate picture of what it was like to be president. They thought he sat in the Oval Office, pushed buttons, and received instant responses: people snapped to attention; government agencies swung into action; fleets of planes and ships were dispatched to the far corners of the globe. Instead, Truman wrote in his inimitable style: "Being president is spending all your damned time having to convince people to do things you shouldn't have to convince them to do." And so it is for all chief executives.

★ ★ ★ ★ ★

PART TWO
GUBERNATORIAL ROLES

★　★　★　★　★

Overview

Governors play many roles. As leaders, they play strategic roles in articulating values and visions, setting overall direction and priorities, marshalling resources, and motivating support. As managers, they play more operational roles in developing plans and systems for getting results and in orchestrating the financial, capital, and human resources of state government to produce those results.

In this part, seven governors describe their roles—some focusing on leadership, others emphasizing management, all acknowledging the importance of both. Individually, they reveal much about themselves, both philosophically and stylistically. In the aggregate, they provide a panorama of perspectives and insights about gubernatorial leadership and management.

Tennessee Governor Lamar Alexander illustrates, through analogies, what governors do. He characterizes the governor's job as seeing urgent needs, developing strategies to meet them, and persuading at least half of the people that the governor is right. He sees the best governors as making fundamental changes and making them "stick."

Vermont Governor Madeleine Kunin agrees that the reason for governing is to create fundamental social change. She identifies "agenda shaping" as the greatest power of a governor and defines governing as the articulation of a vision and the development of a course of action to achieve it.

Florida Governor Bob Graham identifies the need for a "magical vision," a sense of the future and a higher level of attaining a goal. He outlines the elements of strong political leadership and provides several cautions about the politics of magical vision.

On that theme, Missouri Governor John Ashcroft distinguishes politics as "the art of the possible" from leadership as "the art of redefining the possible." He identifies qualities of real leaders, sees leadership as inherently faith-oriented and focusing on the "horizon," and urges governors to limit agendas.

Kansas Governor John Carlin identifies two primary gubernatorial roles, as administrator and leader, both requiring effective communication. In addition to offering some general guidelines for gubernatorial success and some specific suggestions for effective administration, Governor Carlin illustrates the use and value of good communication in several of the major issues he confronted.

Governor Richard Celeste likens himself to the chief executive officer (CEO) of "Ohio, Inc.," outlines the strategic elements of that executive role, and recounts his experience in playing that role—exerting budget discipline, recruiting managers, and managing crises (namely, closing the savings and loans). He draws essential lessons from that experience and offers practical advice for governors as public sector CEOs.

Likewise, Governor Victor Atiyeh characterizes his role as "president of Oregon's largest corporation," drawing similarities and differences with corporate counterparts. While seeing leadership and management as halves of the job, he surmises that managing may be the more important half. He illustrates his use of sound business management techniques, borrowed from his own experience and that of others in the private sector.

From these essays on gubernatorial roles, several common elements emerge. Both leadership and management are needed from governors. A governor must articulate a clear agenda, one that should be limited. The roles of governors are comparable to corporate CEOs, despite major differences in environment (e.g., public scrutiny, politics, the press) and in structure (i.e., legislators being the board of directors and the citizens being shareholders and customers). Like their corporate counterparts, governors need to focus attention both outward, to identify urgent needs and garner support, and inward, to build teamwork and motivate perform- ance. In that way, both leadership and management are provided, balanced, and integrated.

Governor Lamar Alexander
★ Tennessee ★

Governor Alexander is president of the University of
Tennessee, which is headquartered in Knoxville. He served as
the Republican governor of Tennessee from 1979 to 1987. He
was Tennessee's first governor to be elected to successive
four-year terms. He served as chairman of NGA in 1985-86
and organized the fifty-state education survey, Time For
Results: The Governors' 1991 Report on Education. In
1988 the Education Commission of the States gave him the
James B. Conant award for distinguished national leadership
in education.

The governor is a graduate of Vanderbilt University and
New York University School of Law. In addition to the private
practice of law, Governor Alexander's professional public service
career has included serving as legislative assistant to Senator
Howard Baker (R-Tennessee) and as executive assistant to
the White House counselor in charge of congressional relations
with the Nixon administration.

His remarks as a gubernatorial fellow were made at Duke
University on April 2, 1986.

What Do Governors Do?

Do you remember when Roger Mudd, on national television in 1980, asked Senator Ted Kennedy, "Why do you want to be president?" Senator Kennedy stumbled and fumbled, tried to answer that question and couldn't, and a short time later quit the presidential campaign. When I was getting ready to run for governor in 1978, my wife kept asking me that same kind of question: "Why do you want to be governor?" I found that in order to answer that question, I had to answer the question "What do governors do?"

There are lots of opinions about what governors really do. Take the Manchester, Tennessee, kindergarten students who were asked, "Who is our governor, and what does he do?" This was after I had been in office for seven years. One child said, "I can't think of his name, but we'll call him George Washington."

"What does he do?"

"He talks to people."

Another said, "He owns the school."

Still others said: "He asks people to vote for him." "Keeps the city clean." "He comes to visit us, I don't know why he comes to visit us." "He talks a lot."

The one I liked best was: "He rules the world."

I told Eric, a fifth-grader, this, and he wrote me: "Dear Governor Alexander: If I were Governor, I would never argue with the people. I would not rule the earth, I would be nice. Love, Eric."

Bobby Bradshaw, who is in the third grade in Mrs. Schwepfinger's room in Roane County, wrote me exactly what a governor should do: "If I were governor in Tennessee, I would have the streets cleaned up with a third of the tax money. Then I would take a fourth of the tax money and try to stop acid rain. I would take another part of the taxes and pay the teachers better. After I did all those things, I would probably feel drowsy, so I would go to sleep. After I woke up, I would use the rest of the taxes to make banks and railroads safer places. After there was more tax money, I would clean up toxic waste."

Some people think of the governor as head of state, visiting and smiling and receiving; or as commander in chief, leaping out of helicopters and pulling the cords on those loud guns at the National Guard camps; or as lobbyists—like I was doing at noon today—trying to persuade a recalcitrant senator that if he had the state's best interests at heart he would vote to get our little bill out of committee. As a politician, saying shrewd and compelling things that wipe out the other side. As cheerleader, urging the state on to bigger and better things. All those are accurate in a way.

But I like to think of the governor as Count Basie. The Count's obituary in *The New York Times* told this story:

> There was a memorable concert at Town Hall several years ago when a number of musicians, including Mr. Basie, were scheduled to perform in a variety of combinations. A group that included some of Basie's side men was on stage, playing in a raggedly, desultory fashion, when Mr. Basie arrived. The pianist in the combo gave up his seat to Mr. Basie who sat down, tinkled a few introductory notes on the piano, looked up at the drummer, nodded at the rest of the group and, when the combo took off, the musicians were playing as brilliantly and cleanly as they had been disheveled only a few moments before.[6]

When Count Basie was playing the piano, the whole band sounded better. That's true when you have a good governor of a state.

Governors don't really have *accomplishments*. It's nice to say, "Governor Alexander recruited Saturn and brought in $6 billion of investments," but the truth is, that's really not what happened. The state itself attracted those investments. Maybe the governor more than anybody else helped to put the state's best foot forward, but it's more like Count Basie bringing out the best in his band. It's not just a one-man show.

One way to understand what a governor does is first to ask, "Why do we have governors?" The publisher of the Nashville *Tennessean*, John Seigenthaler, gave me a book just after I was elected in 1978. The book was George Reedy's *Twilight of the Presidency*. In it, Reedy gives the perfect definition of what a governor is for. (He's really talking about the president of the United States, but it's the same thing.) The job is (1) to see the urgent needs of the state; (2) to develop strategies to meet those needs; and (3) to persuade at least half the people that the governor's right. That's the best definition of the governor's job I've ever heard and it's one that I've followed scrupulously for the last seven years. For example, I walked across Tennessee in my campaign. That reminded me that Tennessee was a poor state—people need more money in their pockets. That's Tennessee's most urgent need. After a while, I realized that better schools meant better jobs, and that became my strategy. Then I spent most of my time trying to persuade half the people that I was right. Need, plus strategy, plus persuading half the people you are right—that's what the governor is for, so that's what a governor does.

Some governors are better at what they do than others, just as in Japanese karate there are six belt degrees. I would submit that there is such a thing as a "Black-Belt Governor." Some of you may be karate experts, so you know that the belts go white, yellow, blue, green, brown with three degrees, then black with ten degrees. You might think about governors that way.

The first belt, white, would be getting elected; that by itself is a pretty good accomplishment. Next is yellow—for those who can also stay honest. Next is blue—staying popular enough to get things done. Not popular because you want to look good in the mirror, but popular enough to have the political muscle to get things done. Next is green—awarded for "keeping the wagon in the road and out of ditches." Now if you've done all of that, you're a fourth-belt karate-expert governor, and the truth is, you still haven't really done anything except survive.

Next would come the brown belt, which has three degrees. I would say just thinking and innovating would be good enough to earn all three degrees within a brown belt. Finally, the black belt would be reserved for the rare governor who can make fundamental changes in the state and make them stick.

Now let me offer some comments on the meaning of these degrees. The first belt, the white belt, is getting elected. If I were you, I'd disregard most of what these belt wearers say because almost no politician has any idea of why he or she got elected. Now they will all proceed to tell you for hours all of their great strategies, but most have no earthly idea why they won. The only consistent thing that runs through elections is that the winner both started and finished the race. The only thing I know to recommend to improve your chances of winning is to be able to actually answer the question, "Why do you want to be governor?" If you can do that, you will be confident in your own attitudes and ideas and you will radiate that confidence and you will have a course of action. That's really what people want in elected leadership.

The yellow belt is for staying honest. "Well," you say, "why would you even bring that up? That ought to be assumed." I agree. When I walked across the state, a little lady in Hawkins County, Rogersville, Tennessee, wiggled her finger at me in a way I've never forgotten, and said, "I'll tell you how to get elected." I still had about five months and five hundred miles to go to Memphis so I listened awfully hard. She said, "First, don't make any promises. We're tired of all these promises. Second, keep the taxes down, we can't afford any more. And third, behave yourself when you get in there, we're tired of being embarrassed by all these people who get in office." The most important thing most people like remembering about a governor is whether they were proud or not to have him or her representing them.

Trying to do the right thing is also good politics and the most effective way to get things done. In Tennessee, almost every major recommendation I've made to the legislature over the past seven years has passed even though the legislature is two-to-one Democratic, and even though we've made some dramatic changes that some other states never have been able to do. People wonder how that happened. Jim Henry, who's the Republican leader in the House and the Republican state chairman, answers it this way: "We just try to do the right thing. We try to figure out what the right thing is to do and then we present it so well that they don't have any choice."

Is that naive? I don't think so. Let me give you an example. At the Nixon White House I worked for a man named Bryce Harlow. He almost single-handedly gave lobbying a good name in Washington because he was so well respected. He was also President Eisenhower's favorite staff assistant. Mr. Harlow colorfully told me this story:

It was 1954. The Dixon-Yates matter was in full flowering festering scandal.[7] There were allegations of conflict of interest. The fangs of the media-vampires were full out. It became necessary for the president of the United States—Eisenhower—to put out a public statement because the integrity of his whole administration was coming into question. We staff functionaries— Hagerty, Adams, Person, Morgan, and Harlow[8]—had all laboriously contrived to compose an evasive, bureaucratic squid-squirt intended to blot out all possibility of further suspicion. In other words, we'll go on about our business; you all don't pay any attention to THAT. Then we gathered in the president's office where a flushed Jim Hagerty handed Ike our handiwork. We all sat silently as he read every word. Suddenly he threw the statement over Hagerty's head and out into the middle of the Oval Office. Plainly he was M-A-D and showed his famed temper. His blue eyes flashing and his five-star look on his brick-red face, he handed us his best guttural ultimatum. "Now listen here boys," he said. "I'll never put out anything like that as long as I'm around this place. You've got to understand that the right thing to do in cases like this is to always tell the truth. Put out the facts very fast; don't get cute about it. Just say exactly what the facts are and make it as simple as you can and as short as you can. That way, the whole damn mess will blow over and, before a week to ten days, the public will back you up for being honest about it. Do it this way, like you boys have it here, and we'll all be up to our necks in trouble, and we'll deserve it."

We filed out of the office, chastened and embarrassed, but with a lesson in responsible leadership, and one that I will never forget. He was right, by the way. As soon as we got the facts out, the whole thing died away. That, incidentally, is what I urged that Nixon and Stans[9] do with Watergate in 1972. It would have hurt a few people, but it would have saved the presidency.

About all a governor has to do to earn the blue belt—the one for staying popular—is to stay in touch with the people. The only comment I have about the blue belt has to do with polls. I have learned only to use polls for one thing: to try to persuade other people that I'm popular enough so that they ought to respect my position. I try never to develop a position based on what the polls say, because I'm usually trying to *change* people's opinions. If you take a poll on the gas tax in Tennessee, everybody is against it. So I don't propose gas taxes. I propose road programs. And then present the bill. Once people become sufficiently aware of the road program and how it will help bring jobs, they accept what it takes to pay the bill. Staying in touch with people will give a governor the persuasiveness he needs to change minds.

The green belt is for "keeping the wagon in the road." Well, every governor can tell you lots of stories about how hard that can be. Today's a good example. I was a little late arriving at Duke University because just as I was leaving Nashville a senator called to say that he wants to provide the fifth vote to get the road programs out of committee. Some days I'm trying to get the road program passed and a prison riot breaks out or somebody calls from Memphis and says Washington University has offered St. Jude's Hospital $100 million if they'll move from Memphis. Someone is indicted. The children get sick. (Things like that happen to governors, too.) It's like driving a team of mules with half pulling one way and half pulling the other, all with blinders on, and people shooting at you from all sides. If you can just get through that, you deserve a green belt. The job of governor is like dangling from a helicopter over a pit of alligators with all their snouts up trying to snatch you. I asked former Governor DuPont of Delaware what it's like *after* being governor. He said, "It's six months before you wake up in the morning without grabbing the paper to see what went wrong the day before."

The brown belt—for thinking and innovating—doesn't require making anything happen. It is the governor figuring out what to do, then advising or preaching. Figuring out in 1979, for example, that as the United States went into a recession, it would be right to focus all of Tennessee's attention on recruiting Japanese industry. That turned out to be a pretty good idea. We also figured that General Motors might be impressed by the opportunity to put the Saturn plant next door to the Nissan plant in Tennessee. For Saturn, the Nissan plant being there was either the hook or the kiss of death. The state itself attracted Saturn, but also, maybe just reminding the GM officials that they had been complaining for years about not being on a "level playing field" with the Japanese, and saying to GM, "Well, here's one in Tennessee, so come on down and take advantage of being there in the competition." By the mid-1980s, our state had 10 percent of all the Japanese investment in the United States.

Just concluding that it is a good idea to pay more for teaching well is a substantial decision for a governor because three years ago, not one state paid one teacher a penny more for teaching well. Just coming to that decision was important. A few other examples: deciding that some prisons ought to be privately managed; deciding to create two hundred $1 million Chairs of Excellence at our public universities; deciding to allocate twenty-five of those two hundred chairs to Memphis for the University of Tennessee medical units and to keep St. Jude's Children's Research Hospital; and understanding that Tennessee is geographically in the center of things—and the significance of that. It took eight years for that to really hit me in the face. Finally, I saw a photograph of the United States taken from a satellite at night. Almost all of the lights were east of the Mississippi River, and Tennessee was right in the middle of it. Since transportation costs are such a big part of doing business, that fact makes a big difference to Saturn, to Nissan, to Federal Express, to anybody who needs to be in the center of things.

According to the Japanese, as you work up to the higher levels of the black-belt degree, you get to the point where you contribute back to the art of karate and can teach and carry on. I suppose the best governors do that. "Black-Belt Governors," I have suggested, are those who make fundamental changes in their states and then help make them stick. We established a corporate mission for Tennessee state government: Our job is to create clean, strong, and safe communities where children can grow up healthy, receive a first-rate education, and find a good job. For our state to follow that mission has required trying to make fundamental changes: Japanese industry in an inland state; automobile manufacturing plants for the first time; interstate highways paid for by state funds; paying more for teaching well; a better-respected state university.

I mentioned earlier that persuading half of the people that you are right is the final part of a governor's job, and "Black-Belt Governors" need to know how to name things. For example: "Basic Skills First. Computer Skills Next." "Master Teachers. Master Principals." "Governor's Schools. Better Schools." BETTER SCHOOLS instead of "Comprehensive Education Reform." Walk out into the street and ask anybody if they would favor a "Comprehensive Education Reform Package," and they'll be asleep before you can get through the second two words. "Centers of Excellence." "Chairs of Excellence." "Tennessee Scenic Parkway System." Name it right and half the battle is won.

Governors these days who want to try to be "Black-Belt Governors" have a much better chance if they have two terms. This is one reason the southern governors have been coming on so much more strongly over the last couple of years—so many of us now have a chance to serve two terms. I remember being in the office of Governor Buford Ellington of Tennessee in 1970. He was our first governor to serve two four-year terms (they weren't consecutive). Our newly elected Republican Governor Winfield Gunn asked, "Well, how was it? How was the second term?" And Governor Ellington looked tired and he said, "Well, Winfield, the second bite of the apple was not so sweet." Well, that's not my view of it. The second bite of the apple is when you really earn your degrees, when you can move right on up the level of belts that you're working on.

About a month ago, the governors and their spouses had our annual White House dinner. These are very special times. Partisanship melts away and at the end of the evening, the chairman of the National Governors' Association responds to a toast from the president of the United States. It became my turn to do that this year, and I was surprised at how much I looked forward to it. It was almost like turning thirteen. By the time I'd gotten there, I'd already enjoyed it so much that it was hardly an event.

When the time came, what I had to say to President·Reagan was this: "Mr. President, we governors like our jobs. Fewer of us are trying to be senators. Almost all of us think that we have the best jobs in America, except, perhaps, for yours. Because while the senators argue about war, welfare, social security, and debt in Washington, and become ill-tempered about budget cutting, we governors are creating Governors' Schools for Gifted Children, traveling to Japan recruiting industry, pushing exports, improving the schools, finding ways to pay teachers more, and building parkways with our own money—bringing the best out in each of our states."

It all boils down to that: seeing the state's most urgent needs; developing strategies to meet those needs, and then persuading half the people that you're right. That is what a good governor does and no one else can do that in quite the same way.

Governor Madeleine M. Kunin
★ Vermont ★

Governor Kunin was inaugurated in 1985 as the first woman and the third Democrat to be elected governor of Vermont. She has chaired the NGA Committee on Energy and Environment and served as vice chair of the Task Force on Global Climate Change.

Born in Zurich, Switzerland, she emigrated to this country as a child during World War II. She graduated from the University of Massachusetts and earned master's degrees from both Columbia University and the University of Vermont. Governor Kunin has worked as a journalist, author, and college professor. She also served in the Vermont House of Representatives and as Vermont's lieutenant governor.

Her remarks as a gubernatorial fellow were made at Duke University on December 2, 1987.

★ ★ ★ ★ ★

The Rewards of Public Service

A career in public life can be highly rewarding, and governing a state offers major challenges and deep satisfactions. If the frustration of public life is to have your ideas rejected and your ideals thwarted, then certainly its reward is to have your ideas put into effect and your ideals reflected in the public domain.

It has been my experience to have my view of the world—how it is and how it should be—understood often enough to keep me committed to continuing to pursue this profession. Fundamentally, I believe that the greatest reward for choosing a public career is that one does, from time to time, experience the glorious feeling of affecting events. For me, that defines a rich and meaningful life.

As a woman, as well as an individual whose background did not predestine me for political office, that is particularly exhilarating. Timing permitted me to fulfill my definition of a meaningful life through political participation to a degree that would have been impossible had I lived in a different time and place. As a woman and an immigrant, I am a relative newcomer to the system. In my youth, I limited my ambition to an ancillary role—that of pleader for a cause, educator of others, wife of a man who might do important things, mother of sons and a daughter who would play out my ambitions.

It is more engrossing, somewhat more hazardous, but certainly more challenging to play a direct role. As governor, one of the rewards is the ability to effect change, to manage the day-to-day tasks of governing, and to influence long-term policy changes that set a clear direction for the future. The greatest power that any governor or chief executive has is being able to use the authority of the office to shape the agenda. The old-fashioned bully pulpit may have been redesigned with modern lines, but its basic shape remains the same. It provides a fine forum with excellent acoustics.

But is not enough to discover that one's voice is heard as governor of a state. It is necessary to learn orchestration, how to shape and edit the message, or else only cacophony will resonate. In my first three years in office, the major discipline I acquired was an increasing ability to focus my agenda while engaged in the daily task of governing.

The dilemma of how to govern most effectively may be illustrated by the different styles of Jimmy Carter and Ronald Reagan. Carter was accused of being too obsessed with daily details, not leaving time for either himself or the public to concentrate on defining broad public policy issues. Reagan, we have concluded, is great with broad strokes: he knows what he wishes to achieve, and until recently was highly successful in achieving it, but he also lacked attention to detail. Whether matters such as the Contra Aid question got out of hand deliberately or accidentally is for historians to determine. Regardless, he left most of the management to others—a style considered to be worthy of emulation, at least until it got him into trouble.

There is no easy lesson to be learned here. The truth is, in my opinion, that one has to be both a master of detail and simultaneously have the ability to step back, take the long view, and define a course. It is necessary to function on two tiers. The day-to-day problems and crises of government have to be managed; they cannot be permitted to get out of hand. As governor, I must make certain that problems are detected early and get fixed quickly, and that government functions efficiently. If problems run amuck, not only is one's energy drained and diverted, but also the very perception of being able to govern effectively is damaged and the ability to bring about fundamental change is weakened.

But being governor is more than being a good manager who contains crises. A perfect manager does not a perfect executive make. To govern effectively means that the agenda is defined by setting broadly understood goals that are separated from the daily pattern. Without the discipline of that agenda, all issues take on the same tone. Priorities begin to blur. The reason for governing—to create fundamental social change—is lost.

I believe that this process of shaping a political agenda is more than a learned exercise. The agenda that is defined must reflect one's beliefs, has to be the result of some in-depth thinking, and requires time, as well as patience and trial and error—all of which are luxuries in the life of a governor. But over the years I have learned that it is essential to devote time to the creation of substantive ideas while simultaneously managing crises. That need for long spans of concentration is counter to the pace of political life, which is accustomed to dealing with major problems in fifteen-minute segments. A half-hour discussion is considered lengthy.

When I first took office, I was impressed by how wide the net of my responsibilities had become. I was responsible for everything: a flood had to be contained, a bridge built, a budget balanced, people hired, people fired. Whatever happened, if it was on my watch, it was my responsibility.

Preparing for press conferences is a marathon information-gathering session. I suspect that being the first woman in this job had something to do with my need to know all the facts, to be fully prepared. The anecdotal style of a Ronald Reagan is something I could never engage in.

But having all the right answers is not enough. The total is more than a sum of the parts. To govern means to articulate a vision of the future and indicate a course of action to achieve it. That requires careful editing, some imagination, and the ability to connect with the people—to anticipate and share their aspirations.

Since holding office, I have focused my agenda on two specific areas: education and the environment. In 1986 education became the centerpiece of my legislative agenda. I sought to change the method of funding state aid to local communities and to increase the state's financial commitment to education. I attained—with some modification—most of what I set out to do.

My first step was to make the best possible use of the bully pulpit. At no time does a governor receive more exclusive attention than when giving an inaugural or state of the state speech. In my second term, I decided to depart from the tradition that had dictated that such a speech should touch on all the major issues, all the constituencies, offending no one. Instead, I was a tough editor. I focused on education exclusively. To create the fundamental change that I anticipated, I had to capture the attention of both the legislature and the general public. I achieved the desired result. Education became the central issue of the legislative session.

I maintained the momentum gained through that speech by focusing my public agenda on this issue. Most of my speeches in the next several months were concentrated on it. As I delved into the subject in greater detail, I acquired an increasingly deeper level of conviction about the correctness of this issue. Not only was I proposing a change in the funding of education, but I was also confirming for myself and others my reasons for being involved in politics.

If one of those reasons is to bring about social change, equal opportunity, and a better life for people, then education is the single best route to achieve these goals. I deeply believe that to be true. The immigrant experience, coming to this country as a child who could speak no English, a child who felt herself to be an outsider to the system, I learned how to become an insider, an equal player, through access to our education system. I continue to see this route as the most direct one to social and economic equality for each subsequent generation—be they from different countries or different economic strata.

In addition to enacting the legislation, I was able to raise the public awareness of the value of education. On one level, a governor—any political leader—personifies values. I do not think that values can be an overlay, added on to speeches because a pollster indicates that certain values are in vogue. I think values have to be acquired the old-fashioned way—you have to believe in them.

In 1987, in preparation for the upcoming legislative session in Vermont, the central question was how to manage growth. Following an in-depth retreat on this topic, I decided to appoint a blue-ribbon commission entitled "The Governor's Commission on Vermont's Future: Guidelines for Growth." Chaired by the new dean of the law school, Douglas Castle, former Environmental Protection Agency administrator under President Carter, the commission completed a series of marathon hearings around the state, listening to more than 3,000 citizens express their views on the future of Vermont.

In my charge to the commission, I observed:

> The values that define Vermont—a sense of community which permits us to know one another as friends and neighbors, a belief that we exercise some control over our lives, the luxury of living in a healthy and extraordinarily beautiful environment—these values are sometimes in opposition to the rapid changes we witness in parts of Vermont. The foundation for many of these values was our agricultural heritage, and its decline erodes our rural character.
>
> The result is a growing concern that we are in danger of losing the very qualities that make this state unique. Most importantly, I believe Vermonters want to have a say about the future of this state and not be bystanders to change.

The initial response to this initiative has been overwhelmingly positive. Instead of the polarization we had usually experienced in the past, which had sometimes pitted developers against environmentalists, this topic elicited thoughtful responses from all sides. It is becoming clear that most participants want to enhance their ability to manage growth. That is the easy part. The hard part lies ahead—putting together a strategy based on the commission's recommendations that will enable us to handle growth while adhering to a deeply ingrained Vermont principle: local control.

The excitement of focusing on this issue has made me understand more deeply my own role and my ability to shape the future of this state. I believe that both the process of creating a forum for public expression on this subject and the procedure for translating that concern into policy changes are two equally critical phases.

Sometimes the role of governor allows you to mold an idea that is ready to emerge. Without your articulation, however, it might never see the light of day in any decipherable form, and it certainly would not be shaped into action. That creative process is equal to the satisfaction experienced by the artist. The difference between the artistic life and the political life, however, is that the politician cannot luxuriate in ambivalence. In the end, conclusions must be precise—yes or no, right or wrong.

I recall reading a review of a Martha Graham ballet danced by Baryshnikov. After a particularly trying press conference, I found myself envying the choreographer, the reviewer, and the dancer. All they had to do was tease our imaginations. That, in itself, was art. I believe imagination has to be a *characteristic* of governors. It enables us to envision the future, but it is always controlled by what is feasible, possible, and practical.

Increasingly, as I matured in the role of governor, I discovered an interesting and challenging duality in the role of government "insider" versus government "outsider." Some leaders, and again President Reagan comes to mind, have an uncanny ability to retain the outsider status while they are full-fledged insiders. They can join in the attack on the very system they administer. I find that difficult to do. I recognize that as an agent of change, who also bears responsibility for the status quo, I have a dual role: I am both an insider and an outsider.

Leaders who only harangue their staffs, commissioners, and secretaries are ineffective and demoralizing. Yet if they only protect and defend the actions of their subordinates, they are unable to move forward. In reality, changing a bureaucracy in any fundamental way requires considerable energy, persuasion, and even force. The tendency to continue to do things as they have always been done, to defend the status quo, to dismiss new ideas by calling them old ideas that did not work—all these are deeply entrenched patterns. The only way to counteract them is to use the bully pulpit to shake up the system internally and win public support externally. However, focusing on bureaucratic changes can sometimes cause enormous tension, as well as drain strength from other endeavors.

For example, a recent report reviewed our human services agency and its delivery system. Two years ago, I had asked for an internal study of the agency, determined to make some major organizational changes. By the time it was completed, commissioners had settled into their patterns, opposition began to emerge, and I had to make a calculated decision whether or not to pursue the reorganization.

Already having a heavy agenda of legislative issues and being determined to retire a deficit, I decided to modify the proposals into more modest steps. The recent report implied that we had not acted boldly enough.

The reality was that we could not do it all. Had we moved in that direction, education and other issues would have had to be sacrificed.

One judgment that is made in regard to any problem is how deep and encompassing the recommended solution in any area should be. Should one "go for broke" and settle for nothing less than fundamental change, or will an incremental, step-by-step process suffice? No broad policy answers exist because each situation has to be judged on its own merits. In the education area, I first asked for total reform, which also affected local taxing authority—a highly controversial approach that had a Robin Hood flavor to it: taking from the rich towns to give to the poor ones. My proposal was ultimately rejected, but I did receive a change in the distribution formula. Had I not been ambitious in my request, I might not have achieved any results.

Sometimes any solution short of total revolution is called a "Band-Aid." Sometimes a series of Band-Aids do, in fact, work; other times they do not. On the growth planning issue, I believe it will be necessary to shape a broad vision that sets a sense of direction, even if it will not be possible to obtain all the separate parts necessary to make it work, at least not immediately. I believe it is incumbent on governors to define a problem broadly, to place it in a larger context, while simultaneously devising a practical strategy to effect the solution.

The opportunities for governors to take decisive steps are numerous today. I believe we are in a period of state government innovation vis-a-vis the federal government. The Reagan revolution, ironically, has enabled the states, of necessity, to truly fulfill the expectation to become laboratories for change. In my own state, this is most evident in three areas: education, the environment, and human services.

It is the governors of this nation who formed a national agenda for education—one that I believe will be promoted by the president. We created the link between educational quality and global competitiveness— now generally recognized, but not yet fully realized.

State governments have been in the lead on environmental issues, filling a gap left by the exit of the federal government. When not caught in a cross fire of inaction on such issues as acid rain, the federal government has not possessed the will to make tough decisions, to create standards, and to take action. The public, impatient with and anxious about such delays, has focused on the states to provide interim solutions. States are doing so, but not with total effectiveness. I believe that many of these issues—such as acid rain, ozone, and water quality—demand national standards.

In the area of human services, the welfare reform agenda, articulated in February of 1987 by the governors under the leadership of Bill Clinton of Arkansas, is the result of bold state experiments. Vermont has its own program—Reach Up—designed to enable welfare mothers to become self-supporting for the long term by providing education, training, child care, and transportation. Breaking down the barriers to employment is the goal, and we are beginning to see exciting results.

The states are paving the way, but it is my hope that the federal government will do more than applaud from the sidelines. I hope the Moynihan bill[10] will be adopted and that the administration will make a major investment in human services, and thereby, in our economic well-being. We simply cannot waste our human resources: the children who will become our productive labor force, if we give them the chance.

The relationship between the federal government and the states constantly changes, continuing the debate that was initiated two hundred years ago when the Constitution was written. At one time, the federal government goaded the states into action on civil rights, on public education for the handicapped, on equal rights for women.

Today, the states are often prodding the federal government to follow their lead. It is an exciting time to be governor. Visible results can be achieved. The ability to affect the life of one's time, to participate fully in the human drama, is extraordinary. The rewards are sporadic, but they are tangible: a letter, a phone call, a smile, a photograph, and finally, a sense of accomplishment.

But I am also inspired on another level, which is more difficult to explain. It is my personal belief that it is essential to live a life that extends beyond the circumference of one's own existence. Perhaps that is the lesson I learned indirectly at some point as a child, leaving Europe during World War II: Silence offers no protection. I discovered, too, that political decisions are, in some cases, life-and-death decisions. The person who expresses this thought best for me is Elie Wiesel, who said at the time of President Reagan's controversial visit to the cemetery of German soldiers at Bitburg, Germany:

> I have learned that the holocaust was a unique and uniquely Jewish experience. Albeit with universal implications. Not all victims were Jews. But all Jews were victims.
>
> I have learned of indifference, of the crime of indifference, for the opposite of love, I have learned, is not hate, but indifference.

To participate in public life, I believe, is the culmination of our struggle against indifference—our affirmation of belief in the perfectibility of the social contract that binds us together and makes us mutually responsible for our common well-being. It is exciting work.

Governor Bob Graham
★ Florida ★

*Governor Graham currently serves as a Democratic U.S.
senator for Florida. He was governor of Florida from 1979 to
1987. He served as chairman of the NGA Committee on
Criminal Justice and Public Protection, was the lead governor
for NGA in fighting illegal drug importation, and chaired the
NGA Committee on International Trade and Foreign Relations.*

*Governor Graham earned a bachelor's degree from the
University of Florida and a law degree from Harvard Law
School. After graduation, he was with Sengra Corporation, a
family-owned land development firm in Florida. Before his
election as governor in 1979, he served in the Florida State
Legislature for twelve years—four years as a state representative
and eight years as a state senator.*

*His remarks as a gubernatorial fellow were made at Duke
University on September 19, 1985.*

* * * * *

A Magical Vision and
Other Ingredients of Leadership

During the course of its long history, my state of Florida, which is one of the oldest settled places in North America, has undergone a major metamorphosis. For several centuries—as a colony of Spain and Britain as well as a territory of the United States—its status was peripheral. This was true not only geographically, because as a peninsula it dangled off the North American continent, but also politically, in view of its colonial and subordinate status until it joined the Union as a state in 1845.

Florida has also been looked upon as a "mistress" state. It was a place where people came to have a good time or to make a lot of money. Relatively few came to make an in-depth commitment.

Dating from the early 1960s, Florida has moved out of the peripheral shadows and "mistress" role to become what people like author John Naisbitt now call one of the "Megatrend" states, where the issues of the twenty-first century are being played out today: How do you deal with a population in which almost one out of every five people is over the age of sixty-five? How do you accommodate rapid growth in a fragile environment? If the United States had faced the same population gain as a result of refugee arrivals that the Miami area did in 1980 in a period of about ninety days, the population of the states would have increased by more than thirty million people during the same period. This is the scale of the assimilation of people that one community in Florida has met. All those issues are significant national ones as the twenty-first century nears.

During my political career, which includes service as a legislator and governor (1979-1987) during the "mega" years, I have refined my ideas about the nature and problems of leadership and management and how they may be effectively applied during an era in American politics when the electorate is becoming increasingly "a-partisan" and when the states are assuming major new responsibilities.

The fundamental difference between management and leadership is that the former essentially operates as efficiently as possible within a set of given constraints. The latter, which functions outside the traditional institutions, fundamentally challenges those constraints. At its best, leadership attempts to stimulate people to have a higher expectation of themselves as well as their society and to raise the level of what they believe is possible.

One of the constraints on the exercise of modern political leadership is that it is frequently judged in the same traditional ways as politicians often are. For instance, governors' achievements with the legislature are often cited as the litmus paper of their political success. One of the great modern governors of Florida, LeRoy Collins, who served from 1955 to 1961, was asked shortly after he left the governorship by United States Supreme Court Justice Hugo Black what he considered to be his biggest failure as governor of Florida. Collins answered that it was his inability to persuade the legislature, over his six-year term, to reform itself so that its representation would be more consistent with the population of the state. Justice Black said, "Governor, that was not a failure," and then explained why.

In 1962, two years after Collins had left the governorship, the United States Supreme Court was considering *Baker v. Carr*,[11] in which the apportionment of the Tennessee legislature was challenged. Before that case, the Court had taken the position that it was inappropriate for it to become involved in what it viewed as the political thicket of legislative reapportionment. Justice Black told Collins that his tenacious, though unsuccessful, effort to achieve it in Florida had convinced the Court that reapportionment would require judicial intervention. So what Collins thought was his greatest failure, in a broader sense, was a triumph. His leadership on the issue was a significant factor in influencing the Court to initiate the wave of reform that legislative reapportionment has generated.

Besides the persistence and initiative that Governor Collins demonstrated in that situation, what are some of the other elements in strong political leadership? They include independence, self-confidence without arrogance, sensitivity, a sense of vision, and breadth of experience. Some significant changes have occurred over the years in the environment in which political leadership is created. The modern generation has been described as information-rich and experience-poor. Earlier generations lived in a much more rural environment. To be economically self-sufficient, all the family members were required to have a diversity of skills, some mechanical and some human. They were deficient in information but rich in experience. To enhance political leadership in today's information-rich, experience-poor society, I believe that individuals should take various steps.

One of these is to establish an alternative to politics. The most ineffective people I have known in this field are those who have not done so. The stereotype is a man who was president of the student body of a state university. He is elected to his first political position at the age of twenty-six. Four years later, he is elected to Congress. A decade hence, he is defeated in a reelection campaign. Now at mid-life and lacking any other experience except in politics, he faces an economic trauma—and a psychological one as well without the rewards of public service. Because the trauma is so great, these people will do almost anything to avoid political defeat. They give up their political and personal independence because they lack professional alternatives.

It is critical to the independence necessary for political leadership that, before individuals commit themselves to such a career, they establish some alternatives that will meet two tests: provide sufficient income to support their lifestyles; and, even more important, furnish sufficient ego-gratification for them to feel adequately rewarded psychologically. The next step is to acquire as diverse a set of experiences as possible.

In my own case, seeking to broaden my horizons and starting while I was a member of the state legislature, I have taught high school civics in Carol City, sold Burger King hamburgers in Fort Lauderdale, worked as a computer operator in Jacksonville, served as a policeman in Panama City, and will soon play a role in a production of the Florida Repertory Theatre at West Palm Beach.

The political campaign ought to be part of the diversity in learning experiences for would-be political leaders. If I were a journalist interviewing political candidates, the first question that I would ask all of them is: "When did you start your political campaign?" The second question would be: "Since that date, what have you experienced, what have you learned, and what changes have occurred that have made you a better person to serve in the office that you are seeking than prior to that date?" The present trend to dilute political campaigns by limiting the activities of candidates in order to showcase them also deprives them of an enriching educational experience.

Another ingredient of political leadership is a fundamental sense of optimism. Effective leaders must truly believe that they have an opportunity to make things better. In my opinion, a basic liberal arts education provides that optimistic outlook because the study of mankind and its history furnishes a perspective on human origins and achievements. The knowledge that one generation was able to overcome its travails inspires later ones to believe they will also be able to do so.

An interesting question is the degree to which personal lifestyles influence the growth of political leadership on the part of individuals. Many prominent leaders of Western democracy have had a similar lifestyle: intense political activity interspersed with almost reclusive reflection. Thomas Jefferson and Winston Churchill are two prime examples. During those long, quiet periods when they were out of favor politically, they broadened their personalities, accomplished significant thinking as well as writing, and prepared themselves to resume political leadership.

Today it is very difficult to do that. One of my concerns is that modern politicians feel a false necessity to be on stage continually lest they be forgotten and replaced by competitors. Instantaneous recognition seems to vie with the equally instantaneous forgetting of persons and events. Nevertheless, in my opinion, people who seek political leadership ought to look for periods throughout their lives when they can regenerate themselves so that they will possess the resources and reserve to provide the intensity that will be required at other times.

Political leaders also face special problems in the post-partisan period. David S. Broder wrote a book in 1972 called *The Party's Over: The Failure of Politics in America.* Its thesis is that the traditional American political parties are losing their effectiveness—a thesis that is probably even more valid today. A lot is now being written about realignment: movement from one party to another. I believe that a much more fundamental thing is occurring: people are actually becoming "a-partisan." A reporter from the *Aspen* (Colo.) *Times* recently told me that almost half of the people in the city were registered as Independents. In various states, it is difficult to be registered as an Independent and still be able to take full part in political activities because participation in primaries requires registration in one of the major parties or the other. But in my state of Florida polling indicates that a substantial proportion of those people who register in this way do not psychologically consider themselves to be aligned in a partisan sense with either of the parties. The real level of partisanship is much lower than the numerical indications would make it appear.

What new demands are being placed on political leadership in this increasingly a-partisan period? A fundamental difference is that the parties now tend to appeal to the electorate on a two-step basis. They first appeal to a group of elites, which then inform the general public. Traditional partisan politics were built around the formation of coalitions. Today, particularly because of television, the leaders are going directly to the people, bypassing the coalitions and ignoring the original rationale for political parties. What will this new approach require in terms of leadership that can organize and accomplish important public policy goals?

I suggest that the answer is to be found in the phrase "magical vision." This phrase implies a sense of the future and a higher level of attaining a goal that the modern political leader must be able to convey to the electorate. In recent American history, the most magical vision has been that of President John Kennedy, who pronounced in the early 1960s that within the decade America would place a man on the moon and return him safely to earth. The magic of that dream stimulated a whole series of initiatives—technical, scientific, and political—that were necessary to realize it. This sense of a magical vision that goes beyond the traditional incrementalism of politics is a significant part of the political leadership required in the post-partisan period.

Several years ago, under Jess White's leadership, the Southern Common Market concept was formulated as a means to provide a new competitive edge to the region, which sought economic, cultural, and political advancement. The Southern Common Market has become a magical vision of what the South can achieve through cooperation and has spurred a whole series of regional programs. In my state of Florida, we announced two years ago the Save Our Everglades Program. Our vision was that by the end of this century the area would look and function more like it did in 1900 than it does today. This magical vision, within a few years, has sparked a tremendous series of private, local, regional, state, and federal actions.

Some words of caution on the politics of magical vision are in order. First, do not have too many such visions. A key to President Reagan's success during his first term was his very short, specific, and easily understood and communicated agenda. Some people have said that one of his problems during his second term was that his agenda lengthened so much that it lost its crisp focus.

Second, particular magical visions need to be quantified. President Kennedy did not just say that the nation was going to send somebody, someplace, sometime. He pointed to a highly specific goal: a manned roundtrip to the moon during the decade of the 1960s. A magical vision must have sufficient specificity so that people can identify with it, measure it, feel as if it is their own, acquire a sense of ownership, and know when it has been obtained or the degree of the shortfall. Lack of quantified specificity causes the loss of political cohesiveness.

Third, avoid framing magical visions in confrontational terms: winners versus losers. One of the realities of American journalism is that many political writers are frustrated sports writers who want to convert politics into an athletic contest, in which "winner" or "loser" is attached to each participant's name. A key to political leadership through a quantified magical vision is to avoid placing the issue in such a context.

Fourth, recognize the long lead time that is necessary to accomplish a magical vision. Time-consuming policy formulation, legislative and administrative development, communication, enactment, and then bureaucratic institutionalization are required to convert dreams into realities.

Fifth, the magical vision ought to be written down. Visionaries need to have a game plan in black and white so they will not forget the nature of their dreams. The crisis of the moment tends to push aside long-term objectives.

Of course, all change, visionary or otherwise, must be institutionalized because most of it transcends the period of occupation of a political office. Therefore, it is necessary to depersonalize the objective by not allowing it to become the particular object of an individual and by institutionalizing it through placing it on the agenda of those who have a sustaining capacity beyond a limited term of office. John Kennedy knew he probably would not be president when his goal of placing an American on the moon and returning him to earth was met. The institutionalization of this change demanded effective communication: convincing people not only that it was possible, but also that it was in their personal interest.

When I was first elected to the legislature in 1967, because of my interest in higher education policy, I traveled to Berkeley, where I consulted with Clark Kerr, president of the University of California. I asked him what had happened since the end of World War II to propel his university system from what was probably B-plus rank to one of the major intellectual institutions in the world. Kerr's answer was that for two decades the people of California had identified their own personal prosperity as well as their families' futures with the quality and growth of the state university system. They identified the university's goals with their own personal ones.

Kerr also contended that he was appointed as president in conformance with the university's tradition of making a statement as to its status and aspirations when a president was appointed. In the late forties and early fifties when Kerr assumed office, the university had set a goal of world-class leadership as an intellectual institution, and he was a distinguished scholar. For all these reasons, a dream of what was possible became a reality because it was institutionalized.

Concerning any major reform, many groups of people have a stake in the status quo and resist change as well as institutionalization. Virtually every state in the nation is in the midst of a period of major reform in education. The issue is whether that movement is a fad, which will decline at the end of the 1980s, or whether it will succeed in reinforcing the social, cultural, and economic changes that will be made in this country as it enters the twenty-first century. The answer is largely dependent upon whether or not the educational reform goals are institutionalized in groups such as business, higher education, accrediting agencies, and parents. All of them have a sustaining capacity that will go beyond the term of office of any particular political figure.

My final topic is the special challenges that the states now face. From 1935 to 1975, the federal government was the primary source of change in the nation's domestic and social institutions. The states enjoyed an almost European, provincial relationship: as ministerial agents carrying out directions from Washington. They were not thought of as major initiators. During that period, the governors also played a passive role: for the most part, they did not ask many questions and exerted only limited initiative. One of North Carolina's senators today, Terry Sanford, in 1967 authored a volume entitled *Storm Over the States*, in which he discussed their decline. Another book the same year, by Frank Trippett, *The States: United They Fell*, dealt with the same subject.

Since the mid-1970s, a dramatic change has occurred in the origination of domestic policy: The states have become far more powerful in this area. The reasons for this decline of the relative role of the federal government's capacity to lead include such things as internal philosophical divisions, financial limitations, and the preeminence of national security obligations. All these have reduced the ability of the federal government to be the force it had been for the preceding four decades in domestic policy. States at the same time have undergone such institutional reshaping as legislative reapportionment. People's attitudes have also changed—toward a greater sympathy for closer, community-based decision-making processes. The national agenda has turned to issues that had been more traditional state responsibilities, especially economic policy and education.

Because of the tendency to stick to old definitions despite the continuing process of transition and change, one of the issues that the states are now dealing with is the most fundamental question an individual or institution can ask: "Who am I?" or "Who are we?" The states today are also asking themselves: "What are our most relevant roles?"

Today, the states are obtaining different answers than in earlier eras. They recognize that they are not just governments that regulate and provide a specific set of services but are also major economic enterprises. For example, the Florida state government employs more than 100,000 people and has an annual budget of almost $15 billion. No other economic entity in the state is anywhere near that size.

The states are also beginning to express their economic strength not just through regulatory means, but in the marketplace. For instance, the Florida government, in conjunction with other major employers, has set up a series of employer health care coalitions. They are aimed at reforming the health care system not by regulation, but by using the marketplace factors that an institution that employs 100,000 people, and those employers that it can bring into its coalition, can exert upon hospitals and other health care providers.

States are also asking themselves: "How can we build new relationships with the private sector to accomplish our goals?" There is a tendency for government to see its regulatory function as being a screen, which sets the lowest common denominator and discourages cooperation with the private sector. The question now is how the states can be a magnet and try to encourage in all possible ways the highest level of excellence in performance. The Research Triangle Park, in North Carolina, is a good example of state government establishing a new relationship with the private sector, and illustrates the role that the government can play as a catalyst in elevating the quality of economic opportunities for its people as well as the quality of the relationship between the intellectual and commercial communities. In a state growing as rapidly as Florida, we are looking for new, creative ways to foster a strong relationship between the government and developers and to reward superior development.

Despite the increasingly a-partisan trend in American politics as well as the other problems facing state governments, the application of modern leadership and management principles will help make being governor of a state exciting and challenging.

Governor John Ashcroft
★ Missouri ★

Governor Ashcroft has been the Republican governor of Missouri since 1985. He is the 1990-91 vice chairman of NGA and is NGA's lead governor on federalism. The governor has also served as chairman of the NGA Task Force on College Quality and the Task Force on Adult Literacy.

Governor Ashcroft's career has included positions in both academe and government. He was an associate professor on the business faculty at Southwest Missouri State University and has authored two business law textbooks with his wife, Janet. Prior to his election as governor, he served as state auditor and state attorney general. Governor Ashcroft is a graduate of Yale University and the University of Chicago Law School.

His remarks as a gubernatorial fellow were made at Duke University on January 22, 1987.

★ ★ ★ ★ ★

Leadership: The Art of Redefining the Possible

My dream for the state of Missouri is that it will be an environment of opportunity and growth. It should be a place where both institutions and individuals reach the maximum of their potentials. Some people share only half of that dream: individuals should be able to reach their highest potential, but not institutions. I do not agree. Denial of opportunity for corporate and institutional growth restricts that for individual achievement.

The Ultimate Objective

The ultimate objective is a framework, or environment, of opportunity and growth. To attain that goal, leadership is required. That demands an ability to help people redefine the possible. Great leadership has always helped people understand that options were available which had not been previously apparent. Recognizing those options is essential to survival. As the Proverbs say: "Where there is no vision, the people perish."

Lincoln helped America understand that, in the aftermath of war, the victor could succor the vanquished. That option shocked and sundered the nation, but it changed the course of America—and in fact the world. An example is the twentieth-century restoration of Japan and Germany following World War II. Lincoln introduced a new option for healing and growth.

Redefining the Possible

Politics has been defined as the art of the possible. If that is so, leadership is the art of redefining the possible. As leaders, governors must achieve this capability and motivate the citizens to pursue the right opportunities and extend the frontiers of what they are willing to attempt in their efforts to improve themselves and the quality of their lives.

This nation of immigrants discovered a place where dreams became reality, where their children's progress would surpass their imagination. The American dream represents a unique faith in collective progress through individual achievement. Our forebears established a system of limited government consistent with a society that is propelled by private initiative.

Some people say that we have now reached an age of limits and that the odds are against us. What are the chances for job advancement because of the "baby-boom" glut in the job market? Can our children really hope for better lives than ours? Will we be able to afford to help them through college? Will worthwhile jobs be waiting for them at graduation? When this generation retires, will the working population be numerous and prosperous enough to provide the necessary care and support that older citizens deserve?

Some individuals believe that the promise of opportunity has carried Americans as far as it can take them. Today, a "closed" sign marks many former frontiers. Those without vision quiver as they claim that the end of the upward road has been reached.

That would, of course, be a serious misreading of history and of the potential of the American people. Reaping the rewards of opportunity has never been achieved without effort. The self-reliant courage and determination as well as the sheer hard work of our ancestors are legendary as the "Frontier Spirit." That spirit lives on in energetic Americans today as the "Spirit of Enterprise." It is not inextricably linked with starting a business or making a fortune but with having a dream, a willingness to work, and a dogged determination to make the dream come true. And it flourishes because individuals, knowing the past, have faith that an investment of the sweat of their brows as well as the power of their creativity will take them to heights the cynics say no one can reach.

Real leaders encourage, not discourage; they give hope, not preach despair; they urge sacrifice in the name of progress, not complacency in the name of comfort. They dream great dreams; they refuse to lie awake in fear. They map out a journey to expanded capacity; and, perhaps most important, they create an environment in which excellence is the only acceptable standard and in which people are constantly striving to fulfill their potential.

A single dominant resource will control our future: human capacity. The competition in developing the human resource will greatly influence the distribution of other forms of wealth among states and nations. I believe that the only way to succeed in this competition is to awaken all citizens to the opportunities of America and to empower them to take advantage of those opportunities. Expanding potential often begins with the growth of ability—turning "raw" potential into "ready" potential.

That is why I am an education-focused governor. The primary emphasis of my administration is improvement of my state's educational system—from preschool through graduate school. Education is the single most effective builder of ability. Perhaps the best definition of an educated person is that he or she recognizes and chooses from a much broader array of options than other people.

Other benefits of a sound education are well known, but a few of them bear repeating:

• As people become more educated, they usually acquire greater confidence in their abilities. They become willing to undertake increased responsibilities.

• The higher the educational attainment of individuals, the greater their capability in handling complex problems. As this nation moves into the twenty-first century, those who succeed will be those who have the ability to address the complex issues of the new era.

• The higher the collective educational level of the workforce, the more attractive that workforce becomes to employers the state is recruiting. Existing businesses also benefit from the improved quality of the pool of workers available.

The expansion of the collective potential of the people of the state can be achieved only on an individual basis. That is why education is so important. It helps individuals comprehend new possibilities. As a result, if governors are to lead in redefining the possible, education for themselves and the citizens of their states is essential.

An expansion of potential often requires that people adopt different attitudes. Governors must work to free those whose potential is chained by an attitude of failure; and, in this sense, they are responsible for identifying the strengths and weaknesses of their states, working to amend those weaknesses that hinder success but, perhaps more important, encouraging the citizens to understand that they have much to offer.

This concept was sharpened in my mind just a month after my inauguration. General Motors had announced the "competition" for its Saturn automobile assembly plant. Immediately setting out to capture that plant, we called an economic summit, inviting any and all communities interested in submitting proposals for the plant to do so. We encouraged them to assemble creative and attractive proposals, assisted by the state government.

The plant was not located in Missouri. But, in the process of assessing their strengths and determining for themselves what they had to offer an employer, communities throughout the state expanded their understanding of their potential and became more successful competitors in the economic development area. The pursuit of Saturn helped us redefine the possible. As a result, our communities are much more confident of themselves.

Their potential has expanded. They are ready to grow. It is the responsibility of a strong governor to engage with the citizenry in a continual redefinition of the possible.

The slogan with which the United Negro College Fund advertisements close has a haunting quality for me: "A mind is a terrible thing to waste." The central truth is this: Poverty is not the absence of possessions; it is the absence of dreams. Perhaps the most significant initiative I have undertaken to redefine human potential is the Learnfare Program, which I introduced to the General Assembly of Missouri. Chronic illiteracy and lack of education are contributors to unemployment. The existing welfare programs were unable to remove these impediments to getting off welfare. Welfare programs destroy dreams with the drug of dependency. The cycle can be broken by assisting participants to attain a basic education; and, if that is done, the focus of the welfare system is changed from providing a handout to furnishing a helping hand.

Here is how the Learnfare Program would work. People walking into a Missouri welfare office first meet a job officer. The first application to be filed is a job application, not a welfare application. If the barrier to employment is the lack of a high school education—which cuts job opportunities in half—the person is required to enroll in free adult education and work toward a high school diploma. To make the process work, day care will need to be provided for the participants' children, along with a stipend for incidental expenses, and other support services—all in addition to the regular Aid to Families with Dependent Children payments.

A case manager is assigned to cut through any confusion and red tape to make sure that the system prepares the participants for available jobs. If they complete the entire process and are still unable to find work, the state will help provide community-service employment to establish personal records of work habits, references, and skills. These are the most valuable elements, next to basic education, in finding stable employment.

As I had the opportunity to discuss the Learnfare Program around the state, some of its most ardent supporters not surprisingly were the welfare recipients themselves. Suddenly, they were beginning to dream again. A redefined set of possibilities told them they could break out of the chains of welfare dependency; they could improve not only their own lives, but also those of their children. And they could begin to feel good about themselves. Leadership helps redefine the possible.

Leadership is Inherently Faith-Oriented

A mayor of one of the large cities in Missouri proudly displays on his wall a plaque that friends gave him. The plaque, which purports to describe his management style, reads, "READY-FIRE-AIM." I was committed not to operate in that manner as governor. But it is difficult at times to avoid appearing as if I were, given the frequency, complexity, and force of the unexpected and uninvited issues that confront a governor on a regular basis.

No leader can ever know enough to predict with absolute certainty the outcome of a decision that he or she makes. Governors who wait to make decisions until they feel completely comfortable with them will never make them. Leaders gather as many facts as possible and then rely on judgment to determine the appropriate course. But this approach requires that they maintain a faith in outcomes. I have told my staff that we must use our best judgment to make the right decision, and then work as hard as humanly possible to make that decision right.

Henry Kissinger described the process this way:

> Most action must be taken when a leader cannot see his way clearly to the end. What is needed is a curious combination of egomania and humility. If he is too much impressed with the size of the challenge, he does nothing. If he is too little impressed, he gets into trouble. So many leaders think they can take away the curse of hard decisions by doing things hesitantly or by half-measures. There is no reward for losing because of moderation. [12]

Part of the necessary courage is the willingness of leaders to place their ideas in the marketplace of public opinion. One of the latest fads at major sporting events provides an analogy. Someone purchases a beach ball, blows it up, and hits it into the air. For the next few minutes, or even hours, depending upon the excitement of the activity in the playing arena, that ball bounces around touched by hundreds of hands, all of whom put a different spin on the ball. The person who launches the ball initially has no hope that he or she will get it back.

I sometimes feel that my ideas are like that ball. By the time the media, the legislature, and the public have had their opportunity to impart their own spin, an idea may be radically different from when it was first launched. But it may also be far better. Unlike the individual who launches the beach ball at the sporting event, however, I am sure that I will get the ball back. If it has taken a shape that I do not believe is appropriate, I can burst the ball; that's what a veto is! In my view, a veto is the deciding vote. Veto and vote are spelled with the same letters—just a different set of priorities.

The point is this: Without being willing to trust their intuitions, without a faith that unforeseen events will yield the opportunity to ratify well-intended decisions, and without faith that our system of government is a good one, governors would be unwilling to "release" any ideas in the first place.

Leadership involves risk. But the benefit of accepting that risk is the chance to mold a government that seeks to serve, rather than be served. And in the end a governor who is willing to take risks can make a positive difference in the lives of millions of people. Goethe said it better:

> The moment one definitely commits oneself, then providence moves too. All sorts of things occur to help one that would never otherwise have occurred. A whole stream of events issues from the decision, raising in one's favor all manner of unforeseen incidents and meetings and material assistance which no man could have dreamed would have come his way. Whatever you can do or dream you can, begin it. Boldness has genius, power and magic in it. Begin it now.

Focusing on the Horizon

Drivers of automobiles have two basic choices about where they look. They can stare at the road immediately in front of them and base their actions solely on what the driver of the car directly in front of them does. Or they may drive with their eyes focused primarily on the horizon, checking the car in front of them only occasionally and reacting to intervening events as these events cross their path.

Bumper-focused drivers provide a ride that is often jerky, unsure, and filled with moments of panic. The ride with drivers who keep an eye on the horizon is usually smooth, purposeful, and, though it is sometimes necessary to react to another driver immediately in front of them, that reaction is generally smoother and less panic-laden.

Horizon-drivers have a long-distance perspective on their journeys. They see conditions develop early enough to avoid difficulty and sometimes even use the new ones to advantage. The good driver has the long view. So does the good governor. Someone said that a statesman sees the next generation, a politician only the next election. A good governor must see both.

The principle of keeping one's eye on the horizon recognizes that achievements are restricted by the time the state constitutions allow governors to serve. They must build structures and initiate programs to carry on their hopes for their states beyond their times in office. This long-distance view provides the basis on which they can judge the issues that come before them. Inherent in the concept of keeping an eye on the horizon is the idea that a need for action can be "foreseen" when the focus is kept far enough in the distance. Changes in terrain, traffic pattern, and weather can be adjusted by looking far enough ahead—in a sense, by preparing for the future.

Failure to do so exacts a high price. It is now obvious that the economic marketplace is global. Missouri competes with the other states to attract foreign investment and to market its products. Its status as the second largest auto-producing state has provided some success in attracting foreign investment. But it, and certainly other states, are hampered in their marketing efforts by the fact that its higher education institutions have not risen to the challenge of competing in a world economy.

Paul Henson, chairman of United Telecommunications, has said, "Leaders of tomorrow must be internationalists at heart; but higher education institutions continue to teach like isolationists." Less than 7.4 percent of the students enrolled in those institutions today are learning a foreign language. Yet it is becoming clear that our expanding markets will continue to be in Japan, Korea, and Third World countries—where our graduating engineers and marketers have little skill in communicating in the native language. The ability to market American goods and services is diminished geometrically in proportion to our inability to speak and write those foreign tongues.

The Southern Governors' Association reports that, though U.S. technical literature is quickly translated into foreign languages for use in other countries, only 5 percent of such Japanese literature is translated into English. Thus, while we provide the world with the benefits of our research and the fruits of our creativity, we are unable to profit from those of the Japanese.

Governors ought to be encouraging colleges and universities to prepare their students to take a meaningful place—to be competitive—in the world of tomorrow. My eye on the horizon tells me that our educational strategy will determine whether we win or lose in the global economy.

A long view is highly desirable when handling a state budget. When I became governor in January 1985, Missouri had a $300 million budget surplus. When my predecessor took office, four years earlier, he had faced a $250 million budget deficit that required drastic cuts in the state budget, sacrifices by state workers, and diminished state services.

My term began with another crisis, it seemed to me: a crisis of prosperity. We faced the natural tendency of government to spend its resources in times of prosperity to create programs that will involve ongoing expenses, even in times of diminished revenue. The contrast between my predecessor's problems and mine could not have been greater. Yet the fiscal surplus provided us an opportunity to avert the next budget crisis, to end the boom-and-bust, feast-and-famine cycle that had plagued state finances for years.

My position was that state government should have at least as much financial common sense as the average family: it should save in times of prosperity so that money will be available in times of need. This policy is especially appropriate for state governments because the demand for their services generally increases when times are bad and revenues are down. When demand for unemployment benefits increases, the workers paying into the fund are far fewer. I proposed that we establish a "rainy-day" fund as well as a 5 percent cash-flow reserve and take other measures to stabilize the budget. As a result of these efforts, we were better prepared to meet tight financial times.

Government that does not prepare for the future—does not keep its eye on the horizon—faces the difficult prospect of hurting those dependent on its services in times of scarce resources.

Orchestrating Public and Private Sector Efforts

An unfortunate polarization threatens American society: The expensive luxury of adversarial relationships has pitted business against labor and industry against academia. It is a condition we can ill afford to tolerate; competition forces the adoption of team, cooperative approaches for survival. The old myth that government alone can provide all the answers to the perplexing problems that face society is unsustainable. Government alone will never solve poverty; government alone will never significantly reduce unemployment; and government alone will never encourage men and women to reach their full potential.

The debate about the virtues or vices of all-pervasive government is beside the point here. The fact is that government succeeds best when it understands and appreciates the role of the private sector and seeks to form partnerships to achieve worthy results. It is the governor's job to orchestrate the public and private sectors in this effort because the latter should be encouraged to assist in what have traditionally been considered purely governmental concerns.

Research parks have proven their worth around the country as effective vehicles for job creation in high-growth, technology-intensive industries. A successful park is usually a cooperative venture linking higher education, private enterprise, and economic development agencies. In Missouri, we recently invested millions of dollars in two research parks: one concentrating on biotechnology and the other on agricultural research and development. Our partnership depends upon a state-funded site, private-sector ideas and capital, and the research expertise and brainpower of higher education. Because of their impact on job growth, these parks are simply too important for government to develop alone.

I am a lover of music. Many contend that symphonies perform the most beautiful music in the world. It is interesting to watch the orchestra assemble. An assortment of people—some are small, some tall—carry various types of instruments—some are bowed, some blown—to play different notes. Could anything but chaos emerge? But, when the music begins, under the direction of a person who has a clear, coordinated vision of what the combined effort should produce, and when the conductor accepts responsibility for that effort, the "noise" is beautiful.

When I travel around my state, attending meetings, teaching classes in schools, and dealing with concerned citizens, I become more and more convinced that the state can be a symphony. Corporations, institutions, people, and government together play a part in making Missouri a better place in which to live and work and raise a family. The fact that some make odd sounds does not detract from the quality of life in the state but adds to the harmony.

Governors are symphony conductors. They not only ask their "musicians" to rise to their full potential, but also attempt to coordinate the divergent sounds into harmony.

The Governor as Representative of the People

No person in a state is more a symbol of the government than the governor. If government does its job well—providing services and fostering an environment of opportunity and growth—the governor receives the credit; if government seems to be operating for its own benefit without regard for the people it is designed to serve, the governor gets the blame, and rightly so.

In Missouri, all but two of the departments of state government are controlled by the merit system. Civil servants have a tendency to view the governor as "temporary" and to consider themselves as the only really permanent part of government. This attitude makes it more difficult for the incumbent to make a substantial impact on the manner in which government operates.

When trouble comes to governors, and it inevitably does, the public expects them to solve the problem, not defend the situation. They represent the people to the bureaucracy—not the bureaucracy to the people. Unfortunately, governors too frequently embrace problems rather than solve them.

Yet they need the loyal, hard-working effort of all state employees, who are ultimately responsible for carrying out policy. Upon taking office, I began a series of State Employee Appreciation Days, at which top-notch entertainment was provided and one department was honored at each event. I would personally thank the employees for their efforts on behalf on the people of the state. And though my thanks for their efforts were genuine, the appreciation days served another purpose: They tended to make the civil servants more responsive not only to the governor's office, but also to the citizens with whom they come in contact.

As the chief steward of the people's tax resources, the governor has the right and the responsibility to demand that tax dollars be wisely spent and that wasteful programs be cut back or eliminated. And as the people's representative to the government, I was ever on the lookout for ways in which to improve the delivery of service. My administration determined how well government was operating by establishing means of accounting for a program's effectiveness. Some people say that it is impossible to tell whether government is meeting its responsibilities properly. I do not believe that.

For example, consider the case of Northeast Missouri State University, which was recently recognized as one of the best bargains in education in the United States. It is one of the rising stars in higher education. In 1982 some 3,340 high school seniors applied for admission. Four years later, more than 5,200 applications were received for the 1,700 slots available in the freshman class.

Why this change? In 1973 Dr. Charles McClain, the president, instituted a value-added program. Students were tested as freshmen, then again as sophomores and seniors, in an attempt to assess the effectiveness of the university. And as it excelled in its mission, it lured students who were interested in being educated. The feedback of test data was constantly used to upgrade performance.

Believe me, if this can happen in state-sponsored higher education institutions, it can happen in other bureaucracies.

The Need to Limit the Agenda

In his First Epistle to the Corinthians, the Apostle Paul wrote: "For if the trumpet give an uncertain sound, who shall prepare himself to the battle?" Governors must be "trumpets" and give a certain sound. They must exercise their leadership in such a way that the people understand clearly the direction in which the governors intend to move their states. The number of policy initiatives that they *can* undertake is enormous, and the temptation exists to address them all—to "change the world" during the time that the constitution and the people allow them to serve.

But effective governors must limit the number of major policy initiatives they undertake in a given term. Only by maintaining this focus can they avoid a garbled message to the people and succeed in making long-lasting changes in government. Issues of emphasis are usually identified during gubernatorial campaigns.

My primary focus has been on improving the Missouri educational system and its capability for allowing the people of the state to meet their potential. Increased funding, Learnfare, and value-added programs at state universities have all come to the policy front because of my consistent belief than an educated citizenry is the key to our successful future. And I believe that my willingness to concentrate on this area will, over the long haul, be the single most important contribution of my governorship.

To the extent possible, I want Missouri to be a place of recurrent opportunity—economically and socially as well as educationally. When any person in the state gives less than his or her best, all the rest of us are thus deprived. Leadership must create opportunity and inspire the broad attainment of potential.

Governor John Carlin
★ Kansas ★

Governor Carlin currently serves as president of Economic Development Associates in Topeka, Kansas. He was the Democratic governor of Kansas from 1979 to 1987. He is a past chairman of NGA (1984-85), served on the NGA Executive Committee, and was chairman of the Committee on Agriculture.

A dairy farmer by profession, the governor earned a bachelor's degree in dairy science from Kansas State University, and currently is a partner in a private farming business in Smolan, Kansas. He served as a state legislator for eight years, and was elected speaker of the House in 1977, the first Democrat in sixty-four years to hold that post.

His remarks as a gubernatorial fellow were made at Duke University on October 24, 1984.

★ ★ ★ ★ ★

The Governor as Administrator, Leader, and Communicator

My experience in government is that when things are non-controversial, beautifully coordinated and all the rest, it must be that there is not much going on. —*John F. Kennedy*

Today, in the states, a great deal is going on, and those who are fortunate to serve as governors are in a unique position to ensure that this activity results in progress rather than in chaos. The number of issues they are addressing is increasing yearly. As the federal government gives more responsibilities to the states in areas such as social programs, transportation, and the environment, the position takes on a new significance in the federal system.

In carrying out the duties of governor, an individual serves primarily two roles: administrator and leader. Both of them require the ability to set priorities, to make decisions quickly, and to create a plan for carrying them out. A key factor in being successful is the ability to communicate and to make effective use of information supplied by others.

By examining some of the newly emerging as well as recurring issues facing state governments, it is possible to explain how governors fulfill both the roles their offices demand and how communication influences their effectiveness. Specifically, this presentation will examine the nature of the roles of administrator and leader, apply them to major issues in state government, and describe some of the lessons I have learned about carrying out gubernatorial functions. Underlying the analysis of these three topics is the assumption that they all require effective communication strategies.

The Governor as Administrator

Some aspects of the governor's role as an administrator do not differ from the administrative responsibilities of a corporate executive: the traditional ones of hiring and firing, overseeing budgets, promoting the state, or staying abreast of the "competition." But the presence of the press and politics in the public arena makes the administrative function unique.

Every hiring and firing is subject to public scrutiny. A governor has to be able to handle the media attention and strive to make sure that a story is reported correctly. The media are critical for gubernatorial administration. The many challenging regulatory functions in state government today, such as control of hazardous waste, nuclear power, and asbestos, are potentially of strong interest to the public.

The press can play a positive role in publicizing positions or programs, but it also has a natural interest in the negative. If a governor is not careful, stories can quickly become damaging instead of helpful. When a mistake is made, that is what is emphasized, not the dozens of things that are done correctly. Governors who do not understand the power of the press can be in serious trouble.

Additionally, a governor's role as an administrator differs from a corporate CEO's because of the presence of partisan politics—a fact of life in our system. Interest groups, party officials, and legislators all observe and react to administrative decisions. In this day of legislative oversight of the executive branch, any actions by governors can be subject to such a review, and a governor must be sensitive to the fact that the head of an oversight committee might be building a political career around the issue involved. Therefore, it is not just a matter of doing a job well or making the appropriate decision in terms of the governor's interpretation of the public interest. It is also a matter of being keenly aware of the political implications of administrative decisions and being prepared to deal with the consequences. The bottom line is that the public does not elect the CEO of the largest corporation in the state, but they do elect the governor and the members of the legislature—all of whom must be prepared to deal with that reality.

The political aspect of governing also makes it important to communicate intentions clearly. It is easy for everything a governor does to be construed as being politically motivated. Good programs can be defeated if that is the perception among legislators and the public. Although it is impossible to escape politics completely, their effects can be moderated by carefully explaining motivations and presenting programs from the perspective of what is best for the state. I have always subscribed to the theory that good government is good politics. If governors think of the best interests of their states, then they will be on solid ground politically as well.

Asking the reader to keep in mind those two key differences between the private and public sectors—press and politics—I offer the four following suggestions for effective administration. First, a governor must provide consistent and strong direction. That may sound simple, but it is crucial in practical terms. The governor is the head of a vast bureaucracy, and it is a long way down the line to a classified worker in the field who is actually charged with the final step in carrying out a decision. Unless there is a mutual understanding of how an initiative is expected to be carried out, serious problems will occur. Decisions might not reach fruition, the governor's efficiency might be reduced, or confusion might lead to a negative press and to difficulties with the legislature.

That is why cabinet secretaries, members of the governor's staff, the press secretary, and people in the field offices must follow the same script and give the same explanation to the press. For instance, a chemical spill can turn from a simple problem into a nightmare in the absence of a distinct line of authority or a clear understanding of what is going to be done and how it will be handled. Every key person, including the governor, cabinet secretaries, and division heads, must know who is in charge and how the decision is to be carried out. A state senator or representative in the district involved might need to be advised. If everyone is consistent in responses to the press and to concerned citizens, the likelihood is greater that a governor will win the public's confidence in the decision and the problem will more likely be addressed effectively.

My second suggestion is that, in addition to having members of the administration briefed, it is also highly desirable for them to know how to use the media and how to work with the legislature. A cabinet secretary or department head who lacks such capability is likely to encounter trouble very quickly, as is also the governor.

An administrator may be an expert in the technical side of handling an agency and may understand the issues better than anyone else, but, unless that person knows how to keep the press informed or how to work with the legislature, even the best conceived programs can fail. To a large degree, it is the responsibility of governors to see that people working for them understand these realities.

The next suggestion relates even more directly to governors. It is imperative that they back up their administrators and staffs. A perception must prevail among those who work with members of the administration that the governor is cognizant and supportive of what those members are doing. Legislators, lobbyists, community leaders, and anyone dealing with the administration must understand this. A governor makes this a reality by demonstrating support. Obviously, this is possible only when other aspects of good administration are working—primarily a good game plan that all key players understand. The importance of this point is tied to the fact that practically all of state government's work is carried out by someone other than the governor. To be effective, all these individuals must have the gubernatorial clout behind them. When a governor is placed in a position where it is impossible to be supportive of an agency head or staff member, it is time to make a personnel change.

My fourth point is that team effort is required to accomplish the goals of governors. They do not do all the work nor do their agency heads or staff members. Various individuals up and down the line, many of them members of the classified system who have no political affiliation with the administration, are also involved. Many members of the bureaucracy have been in state government longer than the governor or the agency head, and they will be there after an administration is out of office. They ought to feel they are part of the team. They should be brought in and allowed to participate at the appropriate level. They need some sense of being a part of the program rather than just the recipients of orders.

Team spirit is also fostered by demonstrating concern through salary recommendations to the legislature or through communications with agencies. A governor who lets state workers know that their role is appreciated is more likely to foster a sense of responsibility among them.

The administrative role is critical, and a governor will be most successful in that role if there is an awareness of the unique situation created by the presence of the press and politics in the public arena. Those two elements require that a governor provide consistent and strong direction for the entire administration; that its members understand the importance of working with the media and the legislature to accomplish administration goals; that the governor backs up members of the administration and staff; and that a team effort is necessary to fulfill the administrative role successfully.

The Governor as Leader

Although the administrative role often requires governors to carry out the actions of others, the leadership role allows them to address fresh challenges and to provide new directions for their states. Although partisan politics is an integral part of the system, the governor, as a leader, must step outside that role and look at the larger picture of the collective needs of the state. No one else in the government can be expected to take that point of view.

Legislators, by their very nature, represent a narrow viewpoint. Even if 70 percent of the public agrees on a particular issue, that may not be the way public opinion breaks down in a given district. A legislator must represent his or her constituents, even if they represent a minority viewpoint. Thus, only the governor represents the entire state; and through the opportunity to speak at key events in various places, the governor is also the only one who has the resources to carry a message statewide.

As leaders, governors act as salespersons. On some issues, though it is the public who must provide the impetus for action by the legislatures, governors must launch visible, statewide campaigns for support. On other issues, especially those of a complex, regulatory nature, the persuasion must be directed at the legislators and opinion leaders who are involved. Realistically, the issues confronting state government are too numerous to go public on all of them. A governor must be selective. Usually, it is possible to place two or three key issues on the public agenda during a given legislative session. Others are addressed by working with legislative leaders, business leaders, community leaders, and other interested citizens.

If issues are selected wisely, and if they truly represent the collective needs of the state, a governor can incorporate arguments for the key issues into speeches, events attended, press conferences, or monthly television or radio call-in programs. For instance, I identified education as a top priority throughout my administration. Accordingly, my scheduling assistant included as many educational audiences as possible as well as events at which a large number of issues, including education, could be discussed. My speechwriter found ways to incorporate this topic into a variety of speeches, such as those on economic development, the future of the state, or legislative issues.

If the governor takes substantive steps such as these, most citizens can be made aware of how education affects them. Unless that is done, the governor is not going to obtain increased funding from the legislature, especially if new tax dollars are required. Educational quality issues, such as higher teachers' salaries or competency testing for students and teachers, directly affect the public. It is important to let citizens know that, at the same time they are being asked for more money, improvements are being made in the system.

However, by placing the education issue on the public agenda, it was not necessary to discuss all my initiatives in this field. Other issues, such as an internship program for new teachers or the mechanics of competency testing, do not need to be treated in a public forum. They are best handled through meetings with educational leaders, college faculty members who are involved in administering the programs, and public school teachers and administrators who are affected. Through a combination of public and private actions, the necessary leadership to make significant changes in a state's educational programs can be created.

Another example of how to use the public forum occurred in Kansas during the three years I worked for passage of a severance tax on mineral production. For years, a strong oil and gas lobby in the state had prevented this measure. I knew I was not going to achieve my goal by working behind the scenes. Industry leaders were never going to endorse the tax. The pressure had to come from a public realization that a tax was needed for continued financing of essential state services such as education and highways.

I informed industry leaders of what I was going to do, and then I traveled the state with my message. I went public with the idea in December 1980, and I was not successful until the legislative session of 1983. In between, I had to win reelection, but I did so on the severance tax issue. By taking it to the people and by making its importance clear, a powerful lobby was overcome. Tennessee Governor Lamar Alexander has said that governors have a "noisy pulpit," and you can be sure I used it on several occasions while fighting for the severance tax.

In other situations, going public statewide is not necessarily effective. For instance, shortly after I became governor in 1979 I had to deal with the effects of railroad deregulation. Some country elevators would experience severe difficulties if tracks were abandoned. The issue was complex, and it was not one that most of the public was directly affected by. Thus, I did not need a statewide public campaign to gain support for a course of action. Instead, I needed answers to an emerging problem.

My response was to set up a railroad working group representing both the private and public sectors and composed of representatives of the transportation and economic development departments, the utility regulatory agency, and my own staff. I directed them in a semiformal way to coordinate their methods in order to assist communities in addressing the issue. Members of the working group visited with community representatives, railroad officials, Interstate Commerce Commission representatives, and trustees of the bankrupt railroads. At times, members took adversarial positions, but in the end answers were found and railroad lines were saved. Additionally, we were able to work for a change in the state constitution to allow the state to provide financial aid to the railroads. My role was behind the scenes, giving direction to the working group while it publicly assisted those affected in seeking solutions.

The Governor as Communicator

Communication skills are one of the key factors in being successful in both the public arena and behind the scenes. Governors today have to be public-relations oriented, and they must be effective speakers; unless they are good communicators, they will not sell their programs. It is not simply a matter of giving a speech or holding a press conference. The message needs to be carefully formulated. To avoid being caught off guard, it is also important to know the audiences and their positions on the issues and to know what the press has been writing or saying about the issues. The press office should have some sense of what questions will be raised, and staff members and agency heads need to be involved in preparing responses before the questions are ever asked. This preparation will help ensure consistency in public statements by all members of the administration.

Leadership takes many forms, and governors must be aware of what they are. Whether functioning in a public forum seeking support for major legislative initiatives or working behind the scenes with advisory groups, legislators, industry leaders, or ad hoc committees, governors and their staffs must be able to communicate their messages clearly and devise strategies to accomplish administration objectives. Clear communication does not happen by accident but demands research and preparation. The press is an integral part of communicating a message, and governors must recognize its key role and know how to use it effectively.

New Challenges and Old Issues

In both the roles of administrator and leader, a governor addresses a multitude of issues. Some of these change over time and have no precedent in previous administrations or, often, in the governor's personal experience. Others are so basic that they transcend time, administrations, and political parties. Both types of issues require gubernatorial decisions based on the best information available; these decisions as well as the basis for them must be effectively communicated to members of the administration, the legislature, and the public. The following discussion explores specific issues—new and old—that clearly signal just how and why communication is the key to successful gubernatorial administration and leadership.

Regardless of what state or region of the country a governor represents, certain issues will need to be addressed. How these develop and their priority status will be different, but commonalities exist that cannot be overlooked. In recent years, two issues have become of increasing significance to all governors: the environment and the impact of the New Federalism.

The Environment

Environmental issues are not new, but the growing responsibilities states bear in addressing them create fresh challenges for governors concerning hazardous waste disposal and cleanup, nuclear power regulation, and water quality and quantity issues. The nation has learned the hard way that burial of hazardous waste is not an environmentally sound way of dealing with industrial byproducts. Groundwater contamination is one serious side effect, and the cleanup of waste sites can be far more costly than finding alternative methods of disposal.

The issue is both complex and emotional. Governors must consider the needs of the business community that produces waste and has to dispose of it, as well as those of the consumers and the effect of alternative disposal methods on price tags. Governors must also be aware of health risks to current and future citizens. The public and businesses want a solution, but they seek a painless one. However, there is no simple answer to this problem.

In weighing decisions to solve the hazardous waste problem, a governor plays both administrative and leadership roles. Agencies regulating disposal and cleanup must coordinate their activities by keeping in mind the governor's position on the issue. All parties involved—and that can include federal agencies, members of Congress, and the legal community—must be informed about the administration's program.

Additionally, state statutes are not adequate or appropriate for dealing with the problem. This means that governors must seek new legislation. Because of the emotional nature of the issue for those directly affected and the fact that not all communities were threatened, I determined that the problem should not be approached statewide in Kansas. Instead, it required working with the legislative leadership, lining up agency heads and experts to testify before committees, and involving environmentalists and members of the business community in finding solutions that did not put them out of business. All these steps were necessary, and during a recent legislative session we succeeded in gaining passage of legislation to ban the burial of hazardous waste. It was a solution that took time; it did not pass the first time we made a proposal to the legislature, but we were ultimately successful.

The water problem, however, is a different type of challenge in that, with rare exceptions, it is not a front-page headline. Unlike water contaminated by contact with hazardous waste, the problem of water volume is tomorrow's crisis. It is difficult to stimulate interest, either public or private, because few places are actually running out of water today, though shortages exist. Consequently, this is an area that requires foresight. A governor has to be able to look ten to twenty years and more down the road. The real challenge, however, lies in the fact that, though the crisis may be many years ahead, the expenditures to prevent it must be made today. Because of limited state resources, it is not easy to make water a priority.

Success in selling a water plan requires education, which necessitates efficient communication. A governor needs to make the public aware of the volatility of the issue. In Kansas we have done a variety of things to obtain public and legislative support not only for the creation of a statewide water plan but also for its implementation. Several series of public hearings were held throughout the state during formulation of the plan. Maximum effort was made not only for turnout, but also for education through the media. As the plan was being put together, an ad hoc committee of key legislators and water officials was set up to allow regular monitoring of the water agencies. This procedure helped assure ultimate legislative backing, which along with public support indicated that the plan was in the best interest of the entire state.

To complement these efforts, in every economic development speech I gave or in any speech addressing legislative issues, I included water as a basic need requiring protection. This total communication approach is particularly necessary for any challenge that lacks headline "sex appeal." Water fits that description. It is a priority that requires action today even if the payoff will not come until after most current officeholders have departed or many taxpayers are no longer alive to see the results.

Perhaps the most difficult environmental issue is nuclear power. Approximately forty nuclear power plants are being built in the United States today. Kansas has one of them. These plants involve several problems: waste disposal, safety, and cost. Public pressure on governors is intense on all these concerns. And although the federal government has a role in terms of plant construction and safety regulation, governors are responsible for the ultimate security of the citizens. Furthermore, the rates people will pay for power generated by nuclear plants comes under the jurisdiction of regulators who are appointed by the governor.

In many ways, nuclear power plants create situations in which governors are reacting rather than orchestrating. For most of them, the decision to build a nuclear power plant was made during a previous administration, leaving the incumbents to respond to the problems. Constituents flood the office with letters. Protests take place at nuclear plants. Newspapers editorialize. Before acting or reacting, however, governors need to make sure their staffs and administrations have done their homework. This is one scenario that requires both public and private action. Responses must be carefully considered. Multiple players are involved, and the economic ramifications cannot be overlooked.

Most power plants have cost overruns, and someone has to pay for them. Regulatory decisions, in terms of rate requests by the utilities, are one of the biggest areas of controversy in the nuclear debate. While rate hearings are imminent or are in progress, every appointment to a utility regulatory board creates renewed public controversy. Legislative action may be necessary to ensure that both consumer and utility interests are protected, and governors must weigh carefully the part they play in such decisions. None of them wants, nor is it in the public interest, to be a part of a situation in which the so-called "death spiral" occurs. In other words, rates cannot rise so much that consumers cannot afford energy nor demand be reduced significantly. The latter condition only raises rates for those consumers remaining, and the spiral continues. Then, the only way out may be the bankruptcy of the utility, an alternative that serves no one's interest.

In other words, an administration must find a means to protect the interests of the consumer without disrupting the ability of the utility to provide services. Reaching a balance is not easy. Because the issue is so new and precedents are so few, this is a situation in which governors can be of considerable assistance to one another, and it has been addressed at meetings of the National Governors' Association.

The nuclear issue is not going to go away. As most plants go on line, new factors such as decommissioning will face future governors. This requirement will necessitate careful study in the future, and is definitely an issue that will call on a governor's administrative and leadership skills. Once again, effective communication is the key.

The New Federalism

In addition to burgeoning environmental issues, another recent trend in state government is the growth of federalism. When President Reagan advanced his New Federalism philosophy, the role of governors changed.[13] State governments are increasingly responsible for financing social programs and basic state services. That generates the need to scrutinize revenue sources. Governors are being forced to make difficult decisions on tax issues, and many of them have seen the need to raise taxes to cover necessary services. Revenue problems will persist so long as responsibility increases, particularly during difficult economic times. All these factors will test the governor as a communicator.

Likewise, governors have taken a more active role in fiscal policy issues being discussed in Washington. Changes in federal tax laws affect state revenues. Budget-cutting decisions influence actions the states will have to take to compensate for lost federal programs and dollars. Consequently, the governors have prepared policy statements indicating the direction they think the federal government should take on the budget deficit and on tax reform. Armed with these resolutions, the National Governors' Association, represented by individual governors, has testified frequently before House and Senate committees to emphasize those policy positions. Recognizing that it is not enough to sit back and react to what happens in Washington, we must also try to influence the direction New Federalism takes in the states.

Older Issues

In addition to these examples of new issues facing governors, many will continue to be significant regardless of the times. Examples are education, the bureaucracy, and infrastructure problems. Unless states have sound educational systems, they will find it increasingly difficult to attract and enhance business and industry. The cornerstone of economic development is education. All levels, including higher education, community colleges, and vocational schools, must build on the basics established by strong elementary and secondary systems. Not only are good schools vital for children, but business and industry also need the research higher education can supply for technological advances. Community colleges and vocational schools can retrain workers in basic trade skills and crafts when technology alters job requirements. All this is rather basic and obvious, but its emphasis can be lost unless governors stress it when they are communicating with the public.

Education is an issue that must somehow remain in the public arena. Citizens and legislators too often become complacent about topics that no longer generate headlines. The crisis in education today may be on the back burner for news organizations because of a new problem in agriculture or tax reform, but education will always require the attention of governors and legislatures—even before a new crisis stage is reached. Worldwide competition leaves no other choice. Governors can do a great deal to avert crises in education. They need to make steady progress in improving teachers' salaries, instituting higher quality standards for instruction and for teacher training, and ensuring that higher education changes with the demands of a society that will require continual reeducation.

When it became apparent in the summer of 1983 that the nation's educational system was lagging, it was the governors who came to the forefront to provide leadership in solving the problem. A Nation at Risk provided the catalyst for them to take a leadership role in both the public and private arenas and to find innovative means of improving educational delivery systems.

Two other examples of recurring issues facing governors may not be as all-encompassing as education, but they critically affect the functioning of state government. The first is the presence of the bureaucracy. Most employees are in classified systems: they will retain their jobs regardless of who is in office or what party is involved. That core of workers in many ways does not really care who is governor. Nor are they eager to change the way they do things. At times, governors need support from the rank and file to accomplish certain goals, and they had better recognize the built-in resistance that comes from career employees.

Because some problems in state government are never resolved, various individuals in the bureaucracy have worked on them in the fifties, the sixties, and the seventies; and they are going to be skeptical when a governor proposes new solutions or systems. Government employees need to feel they are taking part in decisions. If they lack a sense of participation and commitment, new ideas can die quickly. That is where the governor's leadership role comes into play.

An example of the effect the bureaucracy can have on decision making is a study of the Kansas telecommunications system. Our option was developing our own system or, of course, continuing to lease and buy the services from traditional utility sources. In making a decision, my secretary of administration and I had to rely on input from the experts within the department, people who understood telecommunications systems. As we checked the backgrounds of those individuals, however, we found that many of them had once worked for telecommunications utilities and were prejudiced about the services they provided.

Because of this situation, the decision was difficult. The challenge was to find an objective way to evaluate the information provided by state employees as well as by the utilities. In this case, we turned to outside, private help. But, because we were aware of the problems created by the attitude of our bureaucrats, we were better equipped to find criteria for evaluating the information and to make the best decision.

The second example of recurring issues facing governors is the infrastructure. States have always been concerned with maintenance of roads, highways, and bridges. However, in the past that responsibility has been shared heavily with the federal government, which in recent years has backed away from it, so that more funding is being required of the states. Obtaining that funding is a challenge somewhat like the water issue mentioned previously. Public support does not come until the individual citizen has a personal pothole.

Like education, the infrastructure is a basic need that governors cannot afford to ignore. Because businesses want to locate in areas where they have access to good highways and transportation networks to move their products, governors often must make difficult choices regarding allocation of scarce funds for building new highways or for repairs. Satisfying the needs of urban areas is desirable inasmuch as they contribute significantly to the state's revenue base, but rural areas cannot be ignored. When decisions are made, governors often need to defend allocations for highway funds publicly. And, at this point, administrative, leadership, and communication skills must be merged. Available funds must be properly administered to establish credibility, and additional ones must be obtained.

State government is a dynamic process, even though some elements and structures remain unchanged. Governors must employ their administrative and leadership capabilities in order to handle both new and old issues effectively. Another requirement is the ability to communicate well with members of the administration, staff members, outside agencies, and the public. Governors who possess these capabilities will be prepared for any new challenges.

Gubernatorial Guidelines

Every governor has a personal philosophy regarding the duties of the office and how best to carry them out. Much of mine is influenced by my experience in Kansas. A person can take many steps to prepare for a governorship, but much of what happens can never be anticipated or planned for because issues are constantly changing. Furthermore, changes made in Washington that impact on the states ultimately influence decisions governors make and are often impossible to predict.

Within the framework of these realities, I propose five general guidelines to assist those who aspire to a governorship and to provide insight for students of public administration who study the office. As I briefly discussed earlier, the first and probably the primary guideline for governors is: *Be skillful communicators*. Governors can be brilliant and can have all the answers, in theory, but unless they can communicate well with the public and those with whom they work, they will not be successful. In 1978 I defeated the majority party's incumbent governor, who was a brilliant man. However, his experience and intelligence did not compensate for his inability to communicate with or relate to members of the public. He was not sensitive to the issues they were concerned about nor to the types of solutions they desired.

To communicate effectively, a governor must do several things. One of them is to stay in contact with the public. It is impossible to take their pulse on issues without hearing directly the views of constituents. Communication is a two-way street. It is not enough to make good speeches. A governor must also be willing to listen: to the public, members of the administration, staff members, legislators, and various experts.

The communication function of a governor's office requires extensive coordination. I had to keep my press secretary informed of what I was thinking or doing because he was the one the press contacted for such information. He had to be comfortable knowing that he was truly speaking for me. My scheduling assistant needed to know what my priorities were for a legislative session so that they could be coordinated with invitations for speeches and appearances. If I wanted to promote an education program, then I needed an appropriate forum. My speechwriter also had to be aware of what my positions were on the issues, and to find ways to work them into a variety of speeches. My press office needed to make sure that when I appeared in a city the press knew my schedule and was informed about my availability for interviews. It is not enough to speak to a crowd of fifty or two hundred. Major messages need to be carried to the larger public through the press, and that happens only if the groundwork is laid and scheduling is coordinated with the press office and the organizers of the event.

Furthermore, knowledge about what the issues are in a given community is vital. My agency heads needed to keep me briefed on administrative decisions that had been made that affected a particular community and might raise a question by a constituent or the press. As governor, I had to be on top of what was going on in the state, and I needed to have thought through what my response was going to be before I was ever questioned.

To illustrate what I mean by coordinating the effort to transmit a message to the public, I can explain my strategy when I decided to work for passage of a resolution to allow voters to vote on permitting liquor by the drink in Kansas. Before the 1985 legislative session began, I had to lay the groundwork. I needed to speak before the right groups and arrange some private meetings to make sure that they were supporting me. I talked with and obtained backing from the Chamber of Commerce and state labor leaders before I went public because I wanted to have momentum built up before anyone knew what my plans were on a public level.

I followed up the private meetings with an address to the Kansas League of Municipalities, which was planning to endorse a liquor-by-the-drink amendment. By using a speech to that group as one of my first public forums, I was able to communicate the importance of the issue in terms of economic growth for all communities within the state. I also took into consideration the arguments that would be made by the opponents, and I had my staff construct rebuttals. My press office then issued a column based on my speech to the League of Municipalities, that was sent to all the newspapers in the state to explain my position. My policy office and my constituent service office then prepared a letter that was used to answer concerns expressed by constituents. In the end, we had an organized, consistent message that was communicated in speeches, letters, newspaper columns, and testimony to legislative committees. We were successful in getting the resolution passed, but this would not have occurred had we not carefully constructed the message we wanted to present to key groups and to the general public.

My second bit of advice to aspiring governors is: *Be willing to admit mistakes.* At times, governors must communicate from a less than positive position and need to inform the public and the press that they were wrong. They make too many decisions to be right on all of them. Although courage is required to make a public admission of error, governors are more likely to be perceived as credible and ultimately be successful if they admit mistakes.

This policy may require a governor to fire a member of the administration. On occasion, people simply do not perform as expected. It is better to admit that the wrong person was selected than to risk having a multitude of problems to deal with as a result of the individual's lack of capability. Often such people are friends. They may have been loyal campaign workers. But the bigger picture must be considered .

Perhaps the best example of admitting a mistake during my tenure as governor of Kansas came during the first legislative session of my first term. Although I had been an opponent of capital punishment during my eight years in the legislature, my position when I ran for governor in 1978 was that I would sign a death penalty bill if the legislature passed it. I maintained that by signing such a bill, I would not be an advocate of the position but would merely be carrying out a decision that reflected the will of the people of the state. I was comfortable with that stance during the campaign.

However, by the time a capital punishment bill was passed by both houses of the legislature and arrived on my desk, my attitude had changed. Speaking about the hypothetical and being confronted with a reality was different. It was no longer a debatable position or a philosophical issue, but a matter of life and death. All the reasons I had always opposed capital punishment recurred in my mind and convinced me that I might as well confront the issue head on. I decided to admit to the public that I had made a mistake during the campaign, and that all the reasons that had caused me as a member of the House to vote against the legislation compelled me as governor to veto the bill. My veto was sustained.

Since that first session in 1978, I have vetoed capital punishment bills three more times. Members of the legislature have wanted to emphasize to the public my stand on the issue. But each time I have had the necessary votes to sustain the veto. I paid a price for my decision to admit my initial mistake. When I appeared on television call-in shows, I frequently had to explain why I broke my campaign promise. But the price was a small one when I consider that, by admitting my mistake, I was able to be consistent in my personal philosophy regarding the death penalty; and, in the eyes of many Kansans, I enhanced my credibility because they now know I will admit when I am wrong and do something about it.

My third general guideline for governors is: *Understand that action is what really counts.* Governors have to accomplish something. All the fancy campaign slogans and promises will be of little value if they are not translated into successful programs and legislative initiatives. In the past, a governor could be in office for four or eight years and not establish a major legislative program. But in those times, the economic situation was different, and competition among the states for people and resources was less keen. The states' coffers were usually full, and often the biggest decision involved was which tax relief bill would be promoted. This luxury no longer exists. Citizens want their governors to demonstrate positive leadership. They need some sense that economic development is being promoted, that their children have good schools, that they live in a state that protects its natural resources and maintains basic services.

Governors have to do more than issue press releases, make stirring speeches, cut ribbons, and speak to local civic groups. They must find ways to accomplish what needs to be done for their states. For instance, a governor can provide the leadership to create the finest water plan ever conceived, but, if it is not guided through the legislative process so that it becomes a reality, nothing has been accomplished.

As a candidate, it is easy to criticize what predecessors have done and to unfold a new plan for such things as expanded economic development. But unless governors are able to attract new businesses to their states or provide incentives for existing ones to expand and create new jobs, they are not going to be successful by today's standards. They can be powerful persons within their states if they use both their administrative and leadership powers to translate ideas into action. If they are capable of doing that, then it does not matter if they represent the minority party in the state or even support some unpopular positions. They will be reelected or will put together the coalitions necessary to move programs through the legislature.

To accomplish anything as governor, however, a fourth guideline must be remembered: *Theories do not always work.* Textbooks can be valuable, but there is a limit to how closely governors can follow them and expect to be successful. I have read a great deal about the ideal organizational structure for a governor's office. I can guarantee you that there is no such thing in practice. The only thing that works is to recruit good people. Realistically, the best approach is to assess their strengths and weaknesses and then prepare an organizational chart for those who insist on having one. In other words, do not let an organizational diagram guide personnel decisions; let the personnel guide the shape of the organizational structure.

Textbooks and theories simply cannot keep up with the rapid changes that occur in state government today. I discovered at different points during my two terms that I required a much different set of skills among the people who worked for me. Often that necessitated making personnel changes: shifting people out of my office and into agencies or realigning the structure of the office or revising job descriptions. Flexibility is the key to a successful administration, and it involves the continual reassessment of situations and personnel.

My fifth and final guideline for governors is one I learned from Florida Governor Reubin Askew when I was attending a new governors' conference, and it has served me well: *"Never screw up on a slow news day."* When mistakes are made or bad news needs to be reported, the release of that information can often be carefully formulated and carefully timed. In most instances, a governor has some control over events such as firings or the release of reports and studies containing negative elements. Realistically, there is only so much news every day. If bad news is timed to be released on a Friday afternoon, which is typically a slow time, that news is going to play the entire weekend. However, if the news is released on a Monday, there is less likelihood it will be the top story or will even receive much attention.

Mistakes and bad news, however, cannot always be timed. In those instances, how best to handle the situations to minimize the damage and to reduce public concern must be considered. In some cases, it is best to simply release a formal statement and allow it to speak for itself. On other occasions, that statement needs to be accompanied by a press conference, which allows more opportunity to elaborate on the issue. To some extent, a governor can control the course of a press conference by either having or not having a prepared statement. If the situation is volatile, it is often better to select carefully the initial language by which it is communicated to the press.

The press can be either a strong ally or a source of frustration. To a large extent, how a governor handles the making of news contributes to which role the press plays. This is why selection of a press secretary who understands how the media functions is so important. Equally desirable are staff people who also understand the principle of "never screwing up on a slow news day" because it is not just governors who make news. Others in the administration contribute to its successes and failures.

The above guidelines also reveal the significant role of other people in governors' success. But the bottom line is that the governors themselves bear the ultimate responsibility. Whether it is being an effective communicator, being willing to admit mistakes, or seeing to it that actions by all members of the administration are coordinated, the governor provides the leadership and sets the example.

Each governor has a personal style. Much of what I have related to you about the lessons I learned while serving as governor of Kansas reflect my own. I do think, however, that regardless of the state being governed or the type of personal style, a great deal of common sense is involved in being a governor. And that is gained by being in tune with what is taking place around a person.

Conclusion

The governorship is a unique elective office. A governor represents a statewide constituency, but, unlike a United States senator, is responsible for administering programs and laws that have a direct impact on citizens. The office is an interesting model to study in the field of public administration because of the special position it occupies in our federal system. Governors must deal with a wide variety of issues that require a statewide, and often nationwide, perspective. Because of the nature of the evolving federal system of government, their growing role today includes more direct contact with what is taking place in Washington.

The office of governor has taken on new dimensions in recent years; and, because state government can respond to citizens' needs more quickly and efficiently on many fronts than can the federal government, governors will continue to play a major role in the future of this country.

The modern age demands flexibility from its leaders, and nowhere is that more crucial than at the helm of state government. If governors are to keep pace with this rapidly changing world, it is imperative that they maintain communication with the federal and foreign governments as well as with the governors of other states, with the press, and with their own citizens. Governors who master this skill and couple it with strong administrative and leadership capabilities will serve their states and the nation well.

Governor Richard F. Celeste
★ Ohio ★

Governor Celeste has served as the Democratic governor of Ohio since 1983. He has served as chairman of the NGA Committee on Human Resources and as NGA's lead governor on science and technology.

The governor graduated from Yale University, was a Rhodes Scholar at Oxford University, and subsequently worked in academe, with the Peace Corps, and in the U.S. Foreign Service. Before his election to the governorship, he served two terms as a state representative, was elected as lieutenant governor, and was appointed by President Carter as director of the Peace Corps.

His remarks as a gubernatorial fellow were made at Duke University on October 5, 1988.

★ ★ ★ ★ ★

The Governor as CEO

Shortly after I took office as governor of Ohio in January 1983, I supported a tax increase. The statehouse media promptly reported that I would not be reelected in 1986.

Two years later, on the morning of March 6, 1985, I woke up to the news that our largest privately insured savings and loan was insolvent, jeopardizing sixty-nine other S&Ls in the state. To save the state from an extraordinary crisis in these financial institutions, I made one of the toughest decisions of my political career: to close all seventy S&Ls. The press again predicted my early demise.

The second crisis was so severe that, one year later, *Management Review* of the American Management Association wrote: "Celeste has been damaged politically . . . a 1986 reelection . . . seems a much tougher prospect than it did before the events of March 1985." But in 1986 I was reelected by the widest margin in Ohio's history.

The reason is that real success in dealing with real problems counts more than any political consideration. It always has. It always will. Good governing is the best politics.

This statement is not so obvious as you might imagine.

Historically, the public and the media have viewed a governor primarily as a politician. Reporters—who act as the chief intermediaries between the public and state government—are consumed with politics. They describe each action not in terms of its public-spirited intent nor as part of a pattern of decision making, but in terms of how the voters will respond to it.

Many of us came into government skilled as politicians but untutored as governors. We knew the art of politics; we had to learn the art of governing.

If the days of pure politics in the governor's office ever really existed, they are gone now. The roles and responsibilities of governors have changed dramatically during the last six years. There are too many potential messes—like that of Ohio's S&Ls—that governors are going to have to clean up without much help.

The new reality in state government is that a governor can no longer count on being an old school politician to get reelected. One important reason is the new climate in Washington. Gradually, Washington has let us know that we are on our own. When we call the White House with a problem, we are likely to be put on hold. As states' problems have become bigger and tougher, the federal response has become smaller and weaker.

The Governor as CEO

Good governing *must* go hand in hand with good politicking. Faced with this reality, I have gradually developed a new way of thinking about the governor's role that has helped me put crises in perspective: to be an effective leader, the governor of a state must be as much an executive as a politician. He cannot emphasize one set of skills over the other.

When I took the reins in January 1983, I became the CEO of Ohio, a vast, diversified multibillion-dollar corporation. My operational concerns as Ohio's CEO were not that different from the operational concerns of any other CEO. The budget of the state is bigger than that of Procter & Gamble, Ohio's second largest company. The state's monopoly on workers' compensation would be equivalent to the nation's largest single-line insurance company. Our "gambling operation"—the state's $1 billion lottery—would be the envy of Donald Trump. An annual $2 billion construction budget helps fund highway and infrastructure development and repair. Ohio even manages a $400 million retail operation: its state liquor stores.

Just as a good corporate CEO is never simply a technocrat, neither is a public CEO. The leadership mandate extends beyond the operational to the strategic. The governor must have a vision for the state's future. He must plan for business development. He must make certain that jobs are created. Crises must be solved without losing sight of that vision, that long-term strategy.

I don't want to suggest that a governor will cease being a politician. After all, we are held accountable for our actions more than private sector CEOs. Of course, they must justify decisions to a board of directors—but the board is often chosen by them, and they traditionally have a great deal of influence over it. They are concerned with shareholders. But they have a variety of options—such as leveraging the company to the hilt or taking it private—that a governor does not have.

I do not control Ohio's board of directors and we cannot take Ohio private. My board consists of the ninety-nine members of the Ohio House of Representatives and the thirty-three members of the Ohio Senate. The six million Ohioans who are eligible to vote are my shareholders. They have a stake in what we do and they're vocal about that stake. I am accountable to them in ways that send chills up the spines of some private sector CEOs. (Some companies are now moving toward a fresh notion of accountability, calling their diverse constituencies "stakeholders." Private sector CEOs are learning from the political arena.)

In the end, a governor must balance his accountability to shareholders and their immediate concerns against his or her need to act for both their long-and short-term benefit. Achieving this balance is one of the greatest satisfactions in governing. And in this balance lies the greatest potential for lasting achievement.

The CEO: Honesty, Discipline, and Strategic Vision

When I became Ohio's CEO, I did not inherit a blue-chip company, but one that was teetering on the brink of bankruptcy:

• The state was $528 million in the red.
• More people were out of work than at any time during the Great Depression—about 735,000.
• Our manufacturing and agricultural sectors were in disarray.
• Ohio ranked fiftieth in terms of job creation.
• Ohio owed the federal government $2 billion of unemployment compensation, and was paying millions of dollars worth of interest.
• Thirty-eight of the state's school districts had borrowed state funds to keep their doors open.

Thinking of myself as a CEO as well as a politician was key in helping me map a strategy to solve both specific problems and the underlying difficulties they represented. I learned that a governor-as-CEO must have four elements in any strategy: a clear vision; a strategic plan for achieving it; resources to fuel it; and a strong commitment to leadership capable of rallying the people who make it a reality.

I began with a vision for the state of Ohio, a sense of where we wanted the state to be in eight years. I found the source of that vision directly in the heart of the problem: instead of a state crippled with high unemployment, I saw a state with a job available to everyone who wanted one.

I turned to the state's Department of Development to lead the effort, and to other departments to join in a planning process to address our primary problem: how to create more jobs. First we had to modernize basic industry, then diversify from too much dependency on old-time manufacturing, then transfer technological innovation more rapidly from the laboratory to the marketplace, and finally focus on developing a strong small-business sector.

The second phase of the plan focused on how to use the state's geophysical and natural resources. We began by recognizing that Ohio's location is within overnight delivery of 60 percent of the U.S. population; and that, together with the other Great Lakes States, it is home to 26 percent of our nation's manufacturing facilities and borders on 95 percent of its fresh water. That recognition let us understand we had a location to attract companies, and we aggressively marketed the state.

The plan's third and final phase was a drive to invest in Ohio's human resources, by pushing excellence in education at every level and by placing a stronger focus on community-based human services. As much as possible, we emphasized independence for the communities, from delivering mental health services to reforming the welfare system.

We developed a shared vision, and we quickly came up with plans to implement that vision. What remained was finding a way to pay for it.

We had to make progress in the budgetary area before we could make progress anywhere else. The previous governor had had a very difficult time with budgets and had to choose between acting as a CEO or as an old-time politician. Like those CEOs who leverage their companies to the hilt to fool the shareholders and ward off takeovers, he leveraged the state to the hilt to fool the voters and ward off political failure. He tried to balance the budget—and keep his political popularity—by raising Ohio's taxes twenty different ways in nineteen months, all the while denying that he was doing so. As any CEO knows, however, you can only hide from the numbers so long: he ended up half a billion dollars in the red.

Rather than obscure the need for new taxes, I simply told our stakeholders the truth: we could not hope to accomplish our goals without the necessary funding. If this multibillion-dollar corporation was to become financially stable and competitive—if Ohio, Inc., was to survive as a going concern—the stakeholders would have to invest. So we raised taxes—a managerially sound but politically risky decision. At the same time, however, we provided tax relief for businesses and individuals.

Since I'd been in the state legislature, I was familiar with some of the old ways that governors play with a budget. If, for example, you do not pay your nursing home bills for three months instead of one month, or if you move the last payday into the next fiscal year, you can slide right by a particular point in the budget and act as if you have money when, in fact, you don't.

But that's not how a CEO runs a first-class corporation. In Ohio, we systematically did away with all the gimmicks and passed three consecutive biennial budgets, balanced, on time, and with bipartisan support. In those budgets, we avoided "funny-money" accounting and unrealistically high revenue estimates that force across-the-board cuts once the fiscal year begins. That's the way you brutalize education or hamstring welfare services. We never did this. We even created a rainy-day fund that now exceeds $300 million. It is set aside, protected by statute, and can only be used by a special majority vote of the legislature.

The point I want to emphasize is that I acted as a CEO and imposed the same kind of discipline on state government spending that is imposed in the private sector. Budgetary discipline gives people confidence in the decisions we made about where we're going to put our resources. State employees who administer the programs get confident that they'll be able to run them effectively. And a governor gets confident he'll never get caught short.

Take the budget for Medicaid. Sometimes its budget demands come to far more than we anticipated, even beyond the contingencies we've set aside. Nonetheless, I insisted that we make the cuts necessary to stay within the appropriated figure. As a result, the budget has remained balanced, and Ohio's finances have remained largely unaffected by national economic mood swings.

Starting With People

Good CEOs have to inspire the team of employees that carry out their ideas. That means looking at the state's human resources in a new way to overcome bureaucratic boundaries and manage assets more effectively. An integral part of the success of my Ohio strategy lay in recruiting a special kind of person. In state government, there are always those who say, "We'll do things this way because we've always done them this way." I looked for people who knew how to manage the bureaucracy—not those who disrespected it, but those who understood it enough to motivate it and make it work. I wanted a team that thought change possible and necessary, if never easy.

Of course, every chief executive wants a good team. But frequently the simple diversity of a corporation—the multiplicity of components, most of which do not have anything in common with one another—splinters the vital movement toward a common goal, leaving behind a tremendous waste of human resources. One of the biggest management challenges, therefore, is to unite the departments around a common purpose.

To achieve this maximum effectiveness, we grouped key personnel into "clusters," related groups which cut through and unify the bureaucratic layers. Our Children's Cluster, for instance, was born out of the problem of children with multiple needs. Typically, children who suffer from multiple problems such as physical handicaps and addictions fall through the cracks in the system. Schools can't handle them, human services do not have a place for them, and the juvenile court doesn't know what to do with them.

As a first step, the clusters asked local communities to develop their own cross-delivery programs to help serve children with special needs. The cabinet cluster, for instance, insisted that the local school district in the community talk with the department of human services, the juvenile court, and the rehabilitation services commission. If the local group needed more ideas or suggestions, the case came before the attention of the cluster.

A cluster cuts back on the time it takes to solve a problem. It is one thing when a CEO makes a decision; it is another when the CEO's voice becomes five or ten voices at a senior level, and then hundreds more in the agencies and communities. Too often the decision is never implemented.

The clusters ensure that the administration speaks with one voice, though sometimes it is not necessarily my voice. A special advantage of the cluster is that the group tells me when they think I'm wrong. It's easier with four or five people in a group than in a one-on-one with me.

Saving the S&Ls

An idea like a cabinet cluster is a "systems" solution to an ongoing group of problems. The truth is, however, that no matter what kind of systems an executive puts into place, no matter how many experts rationalize and organize, crises are always going to appear without warning. Things happen when you don't expect them to happen. And you are never prepared.

When some people recount their handling of a crisis, it all sounds so rational. The process seems unusually straightforward: call up the experts; listen to their advice; put your own people on the scene; do not panic. I did all those things during the S&L crisis. But what I remember is not the rational way the crisis played out, but the chaos surrounding it. As someone who was on my staff at that time said, "My primary recollection is of a room full of people screaming. Yapping their heads off at you in meeting after meeting. Phones ringing. Reuters showing up in Columbus. Pure hell." I didn't have a cabinet cluster for the S&Ls.

March 1985 was decidedly grim. When the radio announced that Home State Savings in Cincinnati was about to collapse, images of the depression raced through my mind—pictures of depositors lined up outside the bank trying to withdraw their money. Beginning that morning, I began to learn three difficult but essential lessons for a public sector CEO.

Like so many other S&Ls, Home State had placed too much of its money into an outfit called ESM, a "hot" government securities trader that indulged in massive fraud. This came as news to me, the speaker of the house, and the president of the senate. It was unexpected because, barely two months earlier, we had received a memo from the state's superintendent of savings and loans that said: "There is no need to worry about the crisis in the savings and loans in Nebraska. It can happen in Nebraska but it can never happen in Ohio." The memo had been prompted by a "60 Minutes" profile on problems with privately insured S&Ls in Nebraska. That program sent scores of Ohio depositors to the phones to call the superintendent.

This was my first lesson in the crisis: Bad news seldom travels up. It is a rare person who has the courage to bring bad news to the boss—reality has progressed only somewhat from ancient times when the bearer of bad news was beheaded. I learned that a CEO must work hard to create an environment in which people feel free to air problems. Otherwise, you read about it in the paper.

My second lesson was that when a crisis hits, even the experts want to be led. You will find that very few of those who offer criticisms during a normal time will come up during a crisis with many good solutions to your problems. For a week and a half following the announcement of the ESM failure, I contacted every expert I could think of for possible courses of action. As each option surfaced, however, my staff worried that I was writing my political epitaph.

Even so, I had to do something. Federal Reserve sensors were monitoring "excessive parking lot activity" at the S&Ls as frightened depositors lined up to withdraw their savings. A Cincinnati radio station was telling its listeners: "It's time to panic. Get your cots and tents and line up for your money now before it's all gone." We were in a rapid downhill spiral. Public feeling was near hysteria. In one week, $30 million had been withdrawn; one day later, the tally was $60 million.

After consulting every possible expert I could think of, and weighing the balance as CEO and politician, I made a decision that was managerially sound but loaded with political dynamite: On Friday morning I closed the banks for seventy-two hours. The media prepared my obituary.

As is the case during crises, I tended to work from an overly optimistic set of assumptions, and planned to reopen the banks on Monday. Sunday, twelve hours before the scheduled reopening of the S&Ls, I called their chief executives to the statehouse. There was so much tension in the room, and emotions ran so high, that I was reminded of a high school locker room just before the state basketball finals.

Here were the experts. Their economic lives and reputations were on the line. I reviewed why I had closed the S&Ls and said that they would be legally entitled to reopen in twelve hours, the depositors again lining up for their money. I asked them if they wanted that. When I invited them to speak, a number of executives said they were afraid we wouldn't be able to protect them when they opened their doors on Monday and found the lines of depositors standing outside. At the same time, however, they wanted to be back in business as soon as possible. And they had very little confidence in the federal government's ability to provide insurance in a timely way.

The tension and indecision, coming on top of the Cleveland Federal Reserve's research, showed me what I had to do. I sensed that few of the bankers were genuinely prepared to open on Monday. I said, "Look, I believe I need to have a law passed to require federal insurance. I'd like to get a sense of what your thoughts are. What do you think we should do?"

Most of them mumbled. I asked, "Do you want to open again in twelve hours?" Their response was: "No, not until we have federal insurance." But when I asked if they would put their perspectives in writing—so that in the public's eye, my action would be in response to their request—they replied, "No. Nothing in writing."

One of the executives who had been the most articulate in accentuating that the closing was the only option we had to prevent other institutions from failing said, "Let's give the governor some indication of how we feel. How about all of you who favor staying closed until we can get federal insurance standing up?" All but six stood up.

As they left the cabinet room, these one hundred deeply worried executives were confronted with the kind of television and media barrage with which politicians always contend but with which they were not familiar. Under the glare of the lights, their S&L careers flashing and fading before their eyes, they heard the question: "What did you tell the governor?" To a person, they replied, "We want to remain open. . . ."

We kept the S&Ls closed. I rewrote the executive order that had closed them for seventy-two hours into one that closed them indefinitely. I made no apologies. I acted decisively because I was the only one who had the power to do so. I would do it again if I had to.

Passage of the bill that resulted from the executive order was swift but difficult—like shooting the political rapids. The legislative compromise was hard fought and well forged. It stopped the downward spiral.

While Ohio continued to struggle with this problem alone, aided little by Washington, something unexpected occurred. The dollar started to soften and what had been only Ohio's problem now became an international one. That day, things began to move in Washington. Chairman Gray of the Federal Home Loan Bank Board authorized overtime to help us. Pressed by events, the board had made a policy decision that morning to do everything they could to give what he described as "extraordinary, superhuman" consideration.

I like to term the third lesson I learned during the crisis the "Paul Volcker lesson." It came out of lengthy discussions I had on the phone with the chairman of the Federal Reserve Board. I had never met him in person, but soon came to know him very well. We talked at least once every night for a week. He could not appropriately recommend a course of action; however, he did outline possible consequences of different decisions, such as closing all the S&Ls, keeping only the strong ones open, etc.

He gave me advice, even in the small hours of the morning, when no one else in Washington would talk. And he gave me some straight talk: "Governor, let me just tell you one thing about my experience with financial institutions. No matter how bad the problem looks from the outside, when you get inside, it's going to look a lot worse."

That was not what I wanted to hear at 2:30 in the morning. But he was absolutely on target, and I am glad he warned me. We found a much larger mess than we had expected. We discovered that there were at least twelve institutions that were in worse financial straits than Home State. But we saved the financially sound institutions. We got twenty-seven of them reopened in eight days—which was a record turnaround. In response to our decisive action, the feds did come through. In the end, twenty-six privately insured S&Ls survived as independent entities. The others merged with more solvent institutions. Not a single depositor lost a penny. In 1987, these twenty-six outperformed their federally insured counterparts.

The decisions I made were not the polished results of a long-term strategic plan, but tough choices made with a group of formal and informal advisers working overnight in my office with Girl Scout cookies and milk cartons strewn among the papers.

Both types of decisions came from the same root. They were based on what was in the best interests of our citizens, not on what I hoped would get me reelected.

Faith in the People—Faith in Yourself

As it turned out, the people of Ohio respected tough and honest decisions. Good governing was good politics. People in 1986 understood that I acted, that I took political risks to protect the savings of the average person. People understood that restoring the solvency of the state was the precondition of economic progress.

The decisions we made over the course of the first six years of my tenure have had a positive impact on economic opportunity:

• Ohio is now fourth in the nation in the number of new jobs added.

• Our manufacturing base has again regained its strength; we are first in the nation in truck production and second in autos and steel.

• We have repaid the unemployment compensation insurance.

• Lottery profits rose to $507 million in 1987 from $145 million in 1983.

• Liquor profits have stayed the same despite a $23 million drop in sales over the past five years.

• A number of Ohio schools have received national recognition for academic excellence.

• We continue to make progress in raising standards and expectations about education in Ohio.

State government has entered a new era. Public interest requires that we run our states with the same tough attention to resources and people that characterizes the CEOs of our best-run companies. We are largely on our own. And the lives and livelihoods of our stakeholders are often directly in our hands.

Governor Victor G. Atiyeh

★ Oregon ★

Governor Atiyeh is currently president of Victor Atiyeh and Company, an international trade relations consulting firm in Portland, Oregon. He served as the Republican governor of Oregon from 1979 to 1987, and was the first governor of Arabic descent ever elected in the United States. He was a member of the NGA Committees on Economic Development and Technological Innovation, Human Resources, and International Trade and Foreign Relations.

A private businessman for thirty-five years, the governor was president of a family rug business begun in 1900 by his father and uncle. Before his election as governor, he served twenty years in the Oregon Legislature. The governor attended the University of Oregon.

His remarks as a gubernatorial fellow were made at Duke University on December 3, 1986.

★ ★ ★ ★ ★

The Role of Business Management Techniques in State Government

During twenty-eight years of public service, which included two terms as governor of Oregon, I learned much about the job of governing a state. Being a governor is, in many ways, like running a huge, highly complicated business. I have often said that I viewed myself as president of the largest corporation in Oregon. In fact, if that state were a business, it would rank 102nd among the Fortune 500 — well above any company based in the state and ahead of such prominent firms as Time, Inc., Eli Lilly, and Scott Paper.

Today, governments at every level find themselves grappling with the problems that business has encountered for years. Like their corporate counterparts, the nation's governors constantly face competing demands for diminishing resources. In that respect, Oregon is no different from the other forty-nine states. It is rich in resources, human and environmental. It has vast cattle ranges, fertile agricultural valleys, and millions of acres of the most productive timberland in the world. It has rugged mountain ranges, the stark beauty of high deserts, and the windswept majesty of the Columbia Gorge. And it has people: good, strong, independent-minded individuals who, like their pioneer forebears, know the value of hard work well done.

But Oregon was also hard hit by the recession that struck just a few months into my first term as governor. I never dreamed that I would spend so much of that term — and the one that followed — digging my state out of an economic quagmire. But in government, as in business, the future is hard to predict. And the governor, like the corporate executive, must seize responsibility for using scarce resources where they will do the most good. To do that wisely and well, a governor — like his corporate counterpart — must be both leader and manager.

Defining leadership can be a difficult and puzzling task. To hear the media tell it, leaders are the ones who make the most noise. They stand up on the mountaintop, beating their chests and hollering across the valley about all the terrific things they are going to do for the multitudes below. The television cameras shine on them. The commentators "ooh" and "ah." The editorial writers proclaim: "Now, they're the real leaders."

But, although everyone listens to the individuals who are making all the noise, true leaders head down into the valley itself. They talk to the people who live and work there. They ask them what needs to be done. Then they roll up their sleeves and do it. That is the kind of leader I have tried to be. That is the type I believe all the states need today if they are to regain the energy, vigor, and strength that made this republic great.

The strong government leader and the strong business leader have many qualities in common. In both cases, their job is to turn weakness into strength, obstacles into stepping-stones, and potential disaster into triumph. To do that, leaders must make their objectives clear from the very start. And leaders, be they governors or corporate presidents, must be aware of the realities of their jobs.

One of those realities is the necessity of dealing with the board of directors. In this respect, the average corporate executive has it easy. He or she probably has a board of a dozen or so people who generally see eye to eye. They stop by a couple of times each year, make a few policy decisions, and then go home.

When I was governor of Oregon, ninety people were on my board of directors. They are known as legislators. They meet every other year for as long as two hundred days. Even when they are not in regular session, they may be called in for special sessions to deal with emergencies. They do not just give advice. They wanted to tell me exactly how to do my job. All ninety of them! They kept looking over my shoulder to make sure I was doing what they wanted—or to criticize me if I did not. And, because they came to their jobs with built-in conflicts and differences, they often tried to point me in several different directions at the same time.

I have often mused over the fact that Oregon's government seems to get along pretty well for eighteen months out of every two years. Then the legislature comes back to town, and suddenly we have a new crisis every day. Or at least that is what you might assume from the number of bills legislators write to respond to what they see as crises. And Oregon has it easy compared to states where the legislators meet year-round.

Governors must assert their leadership, even when the legislature is in town. That can be a real challenge. I took office as a Republican governor in a state where Democrats held both the senate and the house. I knew that, at least for the first few years, I would have a devil of a time getting my own agenda written into law. I knew that the Democratic majority would not want to make me or my policies look too good because they wanted to soften me up for the reelection fight.

That knowledge helped me shape my strategies for leadership. I knew these people. I had served alongside many of them, first in the Oregon house and later in the senate. So I made it a practice from the start to meet at least once a week with the majority and minority leaders—though not together. These were private, informal meetings. Sometimes we just chatted about football or golf or fly-fishing. But we also talked candidly about serious issues facing our state. As we did, we established a working rapport.

I cannot say for sure whether that rapport helped me pass one particular bill or another. But it did help keep the rancor to a minimum. After all, it is hard to beat up on someone you know well. And I can say that, during my eight years as governor, I had remarkable success at getting the bills I wanted passed; stopping the bills I was against; and having my vetoes sustained. For example, in the 1983 legislative session, I vetoed forty separate pieces of legislation—a record for the state. All but one of those vetoes was sustained. The point is this: To lead, in business or in government, you must work and communicate with all kinds of people—even those who disagree with you. You cannot let those disagreements turn into vindictiveness. You cannot start thinking of your critics as your enemies.

I know that some people consider the word "politics" to be a synonym for dirty, underhanded, arm-twisting deals. And some of the recent election campaigns, which were characterized by negative advertising and bitterness, did not do much to change their minds. But I cannot agree. If you think arm-twisting is a sound political practice, just have someone take hold of your arm and give it a good, strong twist. It hurts like hell. And it will not change your mind.

As simplistic as it may sound, I believe that the best politics—like the best business—is a matter of doing what you think is right. I contend that the best political strategy is to be as honest and straightforward with your critics and constituents as you are with your close friends. The best political leaders are as quick to admit they are wrong as they are to fight for what they believe is right.

Leadership is only half the job of being the chief executive of a state or corporation. The other half—maybe the most important half—is managing. Somebody once asked the late baseball manager Casey Stengel, "Just what does a manager do?" He replied: "Managing is getting paid for the home runs somebody else hits." To succeed as manager of a baseball club, a business, or a state, you have to recruit some heavy hitters for your team. Then you have to encourage them to slug away with all of their power.

As chief executive, a governor is really just the top manager of a publicly owned business. And a huge business it is. The Oregon state government provides jobs for 42,323 citizens—not counting ninety part-time legislators and their growing staffs. The "corporate" structure contains twenty-six departments, supported by dozens of divisions, agencies, and boards. Assisting them are nearly 2,000 citizen volunteers, who serve without pay on 181 advisory commissions and boards. Clearly, the man or woman who sits at the top of such a complex structure must above all be a good manager.

It helps if a governor enjoys some experience in the business world. I am certainly thankful that I did. Long before I ran for my first term in the Oregon house, I was running my family's rug business in Portland. By the time I became governor and stepped aside as the company's president, I had more than thirty-five years of solid, full-time business experience behind me. I had also served twenty years in the Oregon legislature, where I had learned a lot about state affairs.

That is the kind of background corporations look for when they select their chief executives. In private enterprise, they conduct interviews. They check references. They look for qualifications, experience, and management skills. Government does not necessarily work that way. The state chief executives are elected for a variety of political reasons that may have little to do with experience. Certainly, many who run for office do have strong qualifications. One would like to think those qualifications play a part in the electorate's choice. But when the votes are in, the inexperienced candidate has about as much chance of emerging victorious as the seasoned veteran.

If the victor is not already a good manager, he or she had better be a quick study. Because once the election hoopla is over and the victory speeches are made, you have to get down to the job of governing your state. Managing people and systems is at least half of that job. Governors do not need to be experts on every detail of state government. But to govern well, I believe they must know how to find and hire good people, stimulate them to do their best, and convince them to do the same for their own subordinates.

This is not always easy. Government, after all, is a monopoly. It has the corner on the market. For many of the services it provides, the "customers"—the taxpaying citizens—have nowhere else to turn. Nobody else is maintaining state roads, or running state prisons, or seeing to the desperate needs of the poor, the hungry, and the homeless. It is the governor's job, then, to constantly remind state employees why they are "in business" and whom they are there to serve.

As governor of Oregon, I was responsible for appointing qualified people to many cabinet-level jobs. But, unlike my corporate cousins, I had much less freedom to fire those people if they failed to perform. So it was very important that I find a way to stimulate those under me to do the best jobs they possibly could.

Those in government can learn much about management and motivation from the successes of private enterprise. My own management style grew out of my business background. And I have tried to use sound business techniques to make state government both more innovative and more businesslike. I have always believed that those who work for the state are not dumb or wasteful. I often say that I know of no state employee who wakes up in the morning and says, "How can I waste money today?" These people want to do a good job. They deserve to be recognized when they do.

When I took office, I knew the kind of managers I wanted to help me run the state. I knew the qualities I was looking for. I sought out the kind of people I wanted in the private and public sectors. I told them: "I am asking you to take this job because I know you can do it. I am prepared to give you the freedom to do the job as you see fit. And I expect you to give your best." That is the kind of invitation a good administrator cannot refuse—even if it means taking a pay cut or interrupting a successful business career. It excited them. It told them: Here is a governor who wants to use my talents for the benefit of our state.

Once I had those key people in place, I told them to pass on that same philosophy to their subordinates down the line. Then I went to the other end of that line: to the caseworkers, the prison guards, the secretaries, and the highway crews. I told them: "You are on the front lines. You know how to get the job done. You know how we can do things better. Now tell me."

That was the beginning of Oregon's State Employee Suggestion Awards, a program I am proud to have launched. When a state employee comes up with an idea that saves money, that idea is put to work—and recognized with cash: 10 percent of the first year's savings, up to $5,000 for each winning suggestion. In the six years subsequent to initiating these awards, I handed checks totaling $95,000 to more than 1,200 state employees. Their suggestions are already saving more than $2 million a year. The annual savings are expected to reach $13 million within a few years.

We borrowed other incentives from the corporate world, as well. Special Management Service Awards—but no cash—were given to those managers who did outstanding work for the state or their communities. Productivity Awards recognized outstanding work by smaller sections of state agencies. "Quality Circles" and performance-based promotion and compensation systems were introduced in key state offices. I personally urged my managers to do a better, more positive job of evaluating their employees.

Did these business techniques work? I believe so. When I took office in 1978, I found state government in disarray. Agencies were headed in different, and sometimes contradictory, directions. It was not entirely their fault. They had received no clear guidance from the top.

I recall, for instance, the nursing home director who called me up shortly before I became governor. He was angry and frustrated. A few months before, a state inspector had visited his nursing home and ordered several changes. The director followed those orders, at no little expense. But a few weeks later, another inspector stopped by and told him he had to go back to the way he had originally been doing things. No wonder he was upset.

Well, I sent a clear message to all my state agencies from the day I took office. I told them I wanted state government to run like a business: in an efficient, responsive, cost-effective way. I cannot say that all the complaints have been eliminated. But they are far fewer and less rancorous than they were eight years ago.

Despite the similarities shared by governors and corporate executives, some major differences exist. These may help explain why government cannot always operate the way a business does. For one thing, businesses are allowed to make mistakes. They do, all the time. Those mistakes are rarely aired in public. They are hammered out inside the board rooms and corporate offices. In the process, businesses learn something, become better, and move forward. Government is different. It operates under the constant, critical public eye. It is not allowed to make mistakes. If it does, they are covered in every newspaper and television newscast for weeks and weeks, and politicians hear about them when they are out on the campaign trail.

Even small errors can cost political heads. I still remember how, a few years back, Oregon's largest daily newspaper ran a front-page story about a government mistake that it claimed cost the taxpayers $3,600. The very next day, I presented an award to an employee whose suggestion had saved the taxpayers more than $45,000. I made a point of mentioning the award to the same reporter who had written the story about supposed "waste." The new story was never printed.

As governor, you get used to taking heat for your mistakes and winning little credit for your successes. It comes with the territory. And I would be the last to suggest a return to the days of back-room decision making and hidden agendas. But I know that this constant scrutiny can leave government employees reluctant to take risks. Risks are important. They produce innovation, creativity, and change. They help build the future from the lessons that are learned today. In my two terms as governor, I made a point of telling my people that I wanted them to take risks: "I trust you. Try new things. I am willing for you to make mistakes—and I will stand with you and help you take the heat."

There is one more way in which government and business—and the roles of their leaders—are very different. When a business finds itself in deep financial trouble, it has several options. It can put together a refinancing scheme. It can file for bankruptcy and reorganize. Or, as a last resort, it can shut its doors. I had none of those options. No Chapter 11 is available to state governments. They have no "going-out-of-business" sales. They cannot close their prisons. They cannot reduce their services to the Builders' Board, the Insurance Commission, or the Real Estate Division. They cannot tell the hungry or abused that they are shutting their doors.

Oregon, in fact, has even fewer options than many other states. The constitution forces it to operate in the black. By law, it cannot run up a deficit. And, because its legislature meets only every other year, some pretty fancy forecasting is necessary when the state budgets are planned.

During my two terms as governor, Oregon's economy suffered—as did the state budgets. I found myself forced to call the legislature into special emergency sessions four times to rebalance the budget. Yet we held the line. Our budgets today are providing Oregonians with the same level of services, for fewer real dollars, than they did in past decades.

In the midst of this fiscal struggle, we found time to be innovative, too. The subject of "Workfare," for instance, is much in the news. You may have read about that program in Massachusetts, which is being hailed as a model for other states. Well, Oregon's program is even more successful, no matter how you measure it. The state finds more jobs for welfare recipients each month than Massachusetts does—and at about one-third the cost to taxpayers. More of our Workfare jobs are real, permanent, vocation-oriented jobs that pay a living wage, as much as ten dollars an hour. And all this has been done despite the fact that Oregon's unemployment rate has remained more than twice as high as that of Massachusetts. Our state's Workfare program is based on a simple but important philosophy. We do not say, "We need to get all these bums off of the welfare rolls." We say, "We need to help these people find meaningful work that will raise their independence and self-esteem." I am proud to say that this philosophy is paying off.

Another area of innovation has been in the state's care of its elderly citizens. Everyone knows that the nation is growing older every day. And many senior citizens long for the independence of living in their own homes. But, until recently, the federal government made it very difficult for them to stay home if they needed services under Medicare or Medicaid. Oregon wrestled the federal bureaucracy on this issue—and won. As a result, many of our elders have left the confines of nursing homes and returned to houses or apartments of their own.

Oregon has introduced innovations that benefit business, too. It was the first state in the nation to repeal the unitary system of taxation—a tax that was keeping business out of Oregon. [14] That was a personal political victory for me, and one that illustrates how an understanding of the political process and the people in it can pay off. It was an election year. Everyone told me I was a fool for calling a special session to deal with such a controversial issue. States like California and Florida had tried to repeal their unitary taxes. They had run into real problems. Some Oregon lawmakers were worried that we would wind up with the same kind of mess. But I understood our legislature. I understood politics. I understood timing.

First, I formulated a plan that would treat all corporations equally, whether they were interstate, intrastate, or multinational. Then I announced my plan to the public. I emphasized that repealing the unitary tax would be good for economic development. Only then did I call the legislature into special session. I could have waited until the regular session—but then we would have been putting together a new two-year budget. I knew that, if I gave them my proposal then, the legislators would use the budget process to pick it apart. Instead, I told them: "Repeal this tax now, and I promise that I will bring you a budget next year that is balanced within our means."

I also knew that they all had to be campaigning on their support for economic development, though I sometimes wondered if they all knew what that really meant. I told them: "Look. Here is your chance to cast a real vote for economic development." Well, it took only one day for the two houses to debate and pass the repeal. Of eighty-nine lawmakers present, eighty voted my way. It amazed everyone but me. This story reiterates my point: As a governor, as a manager, you have to know what is going on. You have to understand who you are working with. You have to understand timing.

From the perspective of eight years in office, I would tell future governors this: Pay attention to what the other states are doing. Learn from their successes—and their mistakes. The states are truly the "test tubes of democracy." They are trying new, exciting, and innovative things. Governors who keep track of what other states are doing can save their states money and time.

I would also urge future governors to pay equal attention to the two roles they have to play: leader and manager. If they bring their personal courage, convictions, and commitment to both those roles, they still may not win every fight. But they will be able to hold their heads high, even when times get tough. As Abraham Lincoln said:

> I do the very best I know how—the very best I can; and I mean to keep doing so until the end. If the end brings me out all right, what is said against me won't amount to anything. If the end brings me out wrong, ten angels swearing I was right would make no difference.

★ ★ ★ ★ ★

PART THREE
GOVERNORS IN ACTION

★ ★ ★ ★ ★

Overview

To governors, governing is not an abstraction; it is action. How governors actually govern is best illustrated by case studies.

In this concluding part, five governors describe in a very personal way how they tackled a particular challenge. Other governors face similar challenges. These governors share their particular approach, describe lessons learned, and offer practical advice for others.

Washington Governor Booth Gardner describes a pilot program he introduced as a series of first steps in reforming and restructuring schools, without federal involvement and with only a modest investment of new state resources. A handful of schools were permitted to suspend rules and regulations and to figure out themselves how to use their resources to operate a different kind of school. His hopes in the approach he used are not "model" schools or curricula, but replicable processes for school-based innovation.

Using a very personal, day-by-day "diary" style, Pennsylvania Governor Dick Thornburgh narrates his dilemmas and actions in coping with the Three Mile Island nuclear crisis. He shares the managerial lessons he learned from that experience that could be useful to others, not only in dealing with emergencies, but in handling the more routine problems of governing.

Governor Terry Branstad details a sweeping reorganization of Iowa state government—proposed during a first-term farm crisis and severe budgetary problems—that resulted in avoidance of a general tax increase, substantial budget savings, a priority-driven budget, and, coincidentally, his reelection. He outlines key elements of that process and major lessons learned.

Using a somewhat different approach, Colorado Governor Richard Lamm describes the use of management and efficiency committees of experts from the public and private sectors that helped study and improve the operational efficiency of selected state agencies and functions. He highlights three of those studies, summarizes overall results, and offers recommendations on the use of such approaches.

Encompassing a number of critical challenges, New Hampshire Governor John Sununu shares insights about his own gubernatorial administration and his personal philosophy of governing. He details his early success in solving the state's budget crisis, describes his approach and views on nuclear power and education reform, and illustrates his personal style in selecting personnel and in making decisions.

Although the challenges and approaches in these case studies may differ, certain common themes emerge. Governors *can* get things done despite limited resources and formidable odds. While the substance of the change is important, the process of change may also have a critical impact on the outcome. Those most affected by the change should be involved (such as service recipients, state agencies and other service providers), as well as those who can help build public and legislative support for the change (such as legislative leaders and community groups). Outsiders, and their unique perspective and status, can be invaluable. Getting the fiscal and management "houses" in order can provide both the financial and political "capital" to launch and fuel priority program innovations. Getting results is the bottom line of governing and the governor's own style is the driving force.

Governor Booth Gardner
★ Washington ★

Governor Gardner has been the Democratic governor of Washington since 1985. He is currently chairman of NGA (1990-91) and has chaired the NGA Committee on International Trade and Foreign Relations.

The governor's career has been a mixture of academic, private business, and governmental pursuits. His work in academe included positions as assistant to the dean of Harvard Business School and director of the School of Business and Economics at the University of Puget Sound in Washington. Governor Gardner has served as a state senator and as president of Laird Norton Company. Prior to his election to the governorship in 1984, Governor Gardner was Pierce County Executive.

His remarks as a gubernatorial fellow were made at Duke University on October 7, 1987.

★ ★ ★ ★ ★

Schools for the 21st Century

Impatience and dissatisfaction with schools has by now become almost an undertone in our public life. Parents, teachers, employers, and, as always, students are all critical of the educational system.

I hear of young people who, after twelve years of publicly funded education, are unable to read, or write, or reason their way through everyday problems. Some one-fifth of our children do not even finish high school. There is a great deal of frustration with barriers to student learning and to the freeing of teachers' energies and imagination. Who is at fault? My constituents place blame on two factors. One is resources. The other is the educational system—its rules, its structures, its bureaucracies.

In this presentation, I will describe what I have attempted to do in the state of Washington about the constraints imposed on schools by the educational system. I will not cover the resource question here, not because it is any less important than educational policy. Rather, the resource issue cuts across all the services related to children and families. I have devoted a great deal of attention to the fiscal side. School funding and other concerns related to children and the state's future are the foci of my proposals for tax reform in the state.

The clamor over schools may illustrate the problems in our educational system, but it does have a positive side. It has involved more parents in their schools. It has enabled many creative and dedicated people to think about how our educational system can excel. Not surprisingly, the best of these innovational concepts have come from thoughtful, energetic, and creative people who participate every day in public education: teachers, administrators, parents, school board members, and students.

How should governors become involved in this stormy setting of educational reform? Perhaps a better perspective would be to wonder how they can avoid assuming leadership in some aspect of it. Following is a sketch of the background and course of such reform in Washington State.

Both nationally and within my own state, there has been strong support for major changes in the system of public schools. However, this has not been accompanied by a flow of federal dollars to the states. Instead, the message to governors, particularly in the past couple of years, has been: "Innovate, but with your own resources." Some of the cheerleading from the sidelines called for a major redirection of schools' efforts. Former U.S. Department of Education Secretary Bill Bennett set some lofty goals, wishing, for example, that everyone could read Plato after twelve years of school. Some of the rest of us joined the push for change with fewer prescriptions in mind. In the reform I describe below, the very absence of executive control over specific educational ends makes it not only noteworthy but also attractive to the schools in my state.

What I will be focusing on is political alchemy, or making significant reforms *without* substantial new resources. We have primarily the commonplace materials of politics to produce the gold. First some background.

Educational Reform: National and Local Themes

The dialogue about educational reform in the United States in this decade began with the publication of and ensuing discussion about the report *A Nation At Risk*. Issues related to deficiencies in the ways our educational system operated, our colleges and universities trained teachers, and our students, at whatever level, learned became paramount. As a governor who took office in 1985, during the middle of this intense and often rancorous national debate, I was interested in providing leadership in education and having some impact on the shape of the outcome. During 1986, three reports appeared on the national scene and only reinforced some of my own thoughts on the direction of educational reform in my state. Each of these reports had some influence on our course.

First was the report of the Carnegie Forum's Task Force on Teaching as a Profession: *A Nation Prepared: Teachers for the 21st Century*. In setting the tone for the discussion of educational reform, this task force suggested that in the absence of dramatic change, the American educational system will be contributing to rather than correcting the economic slide occurring in the nation. The plan urged a critical examination of all aspects of our public education system: the recruitment, training, and compensation of teachers, strategies for retaining teachers, preparing minority youth for teaching careers, the emphasis on structure and control throughout the public schools, and the role of colleges and universities in the enterprise of public education. The report specifically discussed restructuring the schools in order to give more emphasis to collegial, rather than hierarchical, relationships and responsibilities. Experienced teachers, working with colleagues, could give the preferred leadership to education's new direction. Also emphasized was a major change in the formal training of teachers: requiring bachelor's degrees in specific arts and sciences subject areas for those intending to teach. Degrees in education would be discontinued at the undergraduate level, but a new Master's in Teaching degree would be established to put teachers on a similar footing with other key professionals in the United States. And finally, a national board would be created to establish and certify high standards for what teachers know and are able to do.

Second, the National Governors' Association, under the leadership of Governor Lamar Alexander of Tennessee, looked to the near-term future in its report: *Time for Results: The Governors' 1991 Report on Education.* It emphasized a trade-off: less regulatory and procedural control by the states in return for better performance by both school districts and individual schools. The report also advocated increased emphasis on teaching as a key profession in our ever-changing economy; a redirection of school management toward shared decisions and a collegial work environment; and a call for experimentation with new technology for instruction as well as with new school calendars and different programs.

Third, the Holmes Group, made up of the deans of schools of education at the country's leading universities, also issued a report: *Tomorrow's Teachers.* It recommended very similar approaches and favored strengthening the education of prospective teachers in colleges and universities by insisting that they have substantive undergraduate majors rather than degrees in education and graduate professional education degrees. Similar to the other reports, this one also called for innovational experiments in individual schools, with more participation by all groups at these levels and much less emphasis on reform imposed from above—whether from the districts or from the state educational bureaucracy.

All these reports were part of the public dialogue nationally and in Washington State through the summer and fall of 1986. Clearly, in terms of the direction of the state's economy and extensive demands for substantial educational reform from all interested groups, this was a time to propose change and innovation. Moreover, a key element in the Carnegie Forum report was its challenge to states and localities to seize the initiative on educational reform. The forum's executive director, Marc Tucker, drove this point home to me and my staff on several occasions as we discussed and analyzed the forum's recommendations.

Two kinds of realities influenced me as we began to think about the tone of our proposals. Major proposals had been made within the state of Washington to reform and restructure the public and higher-educational systems. These had been generated through legislatively created commissions; through recommendations of business leaders; through the office of the state superintendent of public instruction; and through the report issued by the Washington Commission on Excellence in Education, which represented parents, administrators, teachers, and other interests involved in public education.

Public education—both K-12 and higher education systems—receives more than 60 percent of the state's resources. Over 75 percent of the funding for K-12 is provided at the state level—among the highest in the country. Moreover, the head of the Department of Education, the superintendent of public instruction, is an independently elected official who is responsible to the voters and to the State Board of Education for distributing these state dollars to almost three hundred school districts. Educational policy, in reality, is in the hands of the elected school boards in each of these local districts. Much of the public spending is to maintain the system as it is and to handle existing enrollments and numbers of teachers, administrators, and support staff. In the K-12 system, recommendations for major change—substantial increases in teachers' salaries and reductions in class size at all levels—would require the commitment of hundreds of millions of state dollars in additional resources.

However, a second element arose in the fall of 1986 as I was reviewing the budget priorities for state spending in the upcoming 1987-89 biennium. Although I was committed to eventual improvement in teacher salaries and reduced class size in early elementary grades, the projected revenue situation in the state was unfortunately not that congenial. After meeting fixed costs in many programs and accommodating expanded costs already mandated by legislative action in previous years, paying for improvements in our educational system would have to be done incrementally and not through some bold, short-term expansion of the state budget.

Finally, I was influenced and guided by the work and counsel of John Goodlad of the University of Washington and Ted Sizer of Brown University. Goodlad's A Place Called School and Sizer's Horace's Compromise are compelling works calling for change and innovation in our schools.

Consequently, we began to prepare a group of initiatives for legislative action that would usher in a period of change, reform, and progress in public education, but in a more gradual manner than we all would have hoped. In addition to innovative proposals, I believed that we needed to expand programs in those areas that had already proven their worth. The educational package I sent to the legislature thus included an array of programs to meet some of the needs of children at risk of failing at some point down the road. I proposed expansion of efforts for prenatal care, for health and nutrition programs, for beginning a "Project Even Start" to provide services for functionally illiterate parents of children in early childhood education programs, and for an expansion of the state's Early Childhood Education and Assistance Program.

Following some of the suggestions of the Carnegie Forum, the Holmes Group and the Washington Commission on Excellence in Education, I also recommended an end to the undergraduate degree in education, arguing that prospective teachers should obtain an undergraduate degree in a solid subject and then proceed to graduate school for an education degree. To begin to achieve balance on the issue of teacher salaries, I called for the creation of a statewide salary schedule, so that all teachers could earn comparable salaries. Some of these proposals were new initiatives, though some followed earlier approaches that enjoyed considerable support among the voters.

"Schools for the 21st Century": The Proposal

To set the tone for longer-term innovation in the public schools, I made a financially modest proposal to begin creating a new system of education for the twenty-first century. My notion was to pick a handful of schools across the state—a mix of urban and rural, eastern and western, large and small—in order to permit them to start with a blank slate. Traditional state and school district rules and regulations concerning curriculum, school calendars, and so forth could be suspended; and these schools would be allowed to figure out, for themselves, how to use their resources, their staff, their facilities, their parent groups, and their larger communities to operate a different sort of school as they moved toward the year 2000.

Part of my legislative package, then, was a bill in 1987 to create "Schools for the 21st Century" in our state. This legislation was designed to "enable educators and parents of selected schools or school districts to restructure certain school operations and to develop model school programs which will improve student performance." Several assumptions guided this proposal:

• All students can learn.

• Our current schools are overregulated.

• Educators will respond positively if given opportunities to innovate.

• Restructuring the schools is essential to an effective educational system for the future.

• Missing in the professional lives of the teachers is sufficient time—to think, to plan, and to develop new ideas, alone or with other teachers.

• Innovative programs must be concerned with outcomes. Change alone is not the goal. Thus, all our Schools for the 21st Century must commit themselves to some system of evaluation of student progress.

• Parents need to be welcomed back to the schools, and their involvement will provide a necessary and fresh perspective on educational reform. This project was to be our state's commitment to making schools a better place to teach and learn, to enhance student performance, and to improve the professionalism of the staff. The pilot project was to be more than a one-shot experiment; selected schools would participate for six years.

The legislation that eventually passed in June 1987 provided for the appointment of a Task Force on Schools for the 21st Century to assist the State Board of Education in formulating the selection process, as well as in reviewing and selecting the projects. Applications were to be solicited from schools and school districts throughout the state, with up to twenty-one selected as Schools for the 21st Century. Application elements were broadly sketched out in the legislation. It specifically did ask for an expenditure plan and the legislation looked for collaboration with the higher education institutions and relevant groups from the local communities. The legislation also required that all teachers and other staff personnel involved in the project were to be employed for at least ten additional days each school year. Proposals were also to identify those state statutes or administrative rules that should be waived in order to assure some success for the project. Moreover, the state was to assist districts or schools in seeking exceptions, within limits, to those federal regulations that would impede the success of the proposal. To pay for the project in its first year, less than $3 million was needed—a fraction of a percent of state general fund expenditures for K-12 education. This figure illuminates the point that this innovation was attempted in the absence of major new resources.

Establishing "Schools for the 21st Century"

Once the legislation was enacted, I selected prominent individuals to serve on the task force. These were key appointments because they would in large part shape the values and themes surrounding the program. The task force was made up of ten private citizens and four legislators. The ten citizen representatives were three classroom teachers (including a vice-president of the state teachers' union and a local union president); a principal; a superintendent; two deans of schools of education, one from a private and one from a public university; a state PTA officer; a representative of the business community; and a former teacher, currently an educational consultant.

More important than representing various constituencies on the educational scene, these individuals were known to be independent thinkers, unafraid to take risks. When I convened the group for its first meeting, I emphasized that they were selected not only because of their professional positions, but also because of their individual qualities. I asked them to be creative thinkers, visionaries, and problem solvers—not to "represent" a particular constituency. I believe that this was realized, as they showed through their subsequent meetings, deliberations, and very hard work.

The first several meetings of the task force were decisive because in them the flesh was put on the legislation and its intent came alive. The group's first job was to bring to life the values to guide the conduct of the program. As expected, these values evolved not only through extended discussions of the intent of the pilot program, but also by considering the nature and needs of public education in the state. In line with our political tradition in Washington State, all meetings were open to the public, and any citizens who attended had the opportunity to be heard.

Early task force meetings were like seminars, with discussion ranging over all aspects of education. Always, however, the focus eventually returned to consideration of those principles that were essential to the success of the program. Some of the outcomes of these fruitful discussions were the following:

• Application instructions for schools and districts were to be minimal. The task force was not looking for conformity to bureaucratic guidelines.

• Schools and districts were to be allowed maximum flexibility in establishing a format for their applications. Paper and written text were not required; applicants could use video, audio, or any media format. Task force members were to resist giving cues to applicants about a "correct" application.

• Specific proposal evaluation criteria were not predetermined. Unlike most federal or state grant applications, for instance, in ours predetermined scores were not set for segments of the application, such as twenty points for creativity or ten points for a realistic budget. Rather, the task force was to use its collective professional judgment to determine the most promising proposals.

• Schools and districts were not to think of themselves as conducting "educational experiments." Rather, they were to be encouraged to take risks—even to risk failure—with some value placed on creating a setting for innovation, where staff and students would be willing to engage in new activities aimed at restructuring the school as a place for working and learning.

• The goal of the entire undertaking was not to produce "model" schools or "model" curricula that could be exported to other settings, but to encourage and foster the process of school-based innovation.

• Overall, the goal was on innovation to increase student learning and teacher professionalism.

This is the basis of my initiative, the legislation that ensued, and the program that resulted.

At the deadline for applications (late April 1988), 136 schools and school districts had exerted considerable effort in seeking designation as Schools for the 21st Century. They represented eighty-four school districts, or 28 percent of the total in the state. This response was an excellent signal of local commitment to innovation because many schools that submitted proposals said they would pursue their design whether or not they were officially chosen.

Members of the task force read and evaluated each of the 136 proposals; they used individual- and group-ranking techniques to select thirty-one finalists. Representatives from each of these districts and schools met with the task force for an interview. Applicants were not given guidelines on whom to bring to the interview, and the interviews ranged from a superintendent appearing alone to a crowd of seventy-five people broadly representing the school and community.

The task force selected twenty-one proposals and recommended them to the State Board of Education, which approved them. These twenty-one include nine elementary schools, one middle school, five high schools, and six school districts or portions of districts. Two-thirds of those selected are from the western, more populous section of our state; and one-third are from the eastern region. They range from Colton, a small rural school district in the southeastern area, to an elementary school and consortium of twenty-one schools in the Seattle School District, the state's largest.

Examples and Early Achievements of "Schools for the 21st Century"

Following are highlights of the innovations that the twenty-one schools and districts will be introducing over the next six years:

Montlake Elementary School. This school in Seattle will build upon restructuring efforts that have been underway for the past three years to reduce class size, increase the amount and quality of staff development, and reorganize the school day to fit more closely with student needs. Schools for the 21st Century resources will be used to continue the emphasis on restructuring staff deployment to provide small class sizes, teacher teams, extended planning time, and multi-aged student groupings. Collaborative programs with the University of Washington are expected to assist the professional growth of Montlake teachers, as well as benefit the university's teacher-training program. Montlake also intends to take part in a new network of schools that is sharing information on workable new innovations and is making continued improvements.

College Place Middle School. This school, located in Edmonds just north of Seattle, proposes an outcome-based learning model, with specific student achievement goals keyed to standardized math and reading tests. The instructional program focuses on improving academic preparation for high school success, good study skills, enhanced self-esteem, and a capacity for self-directed learning among middle school students. Teachers are now reorganizing the curriculum to emphasize core subject instruction, lasting four periods each day and drawing upon teams of teachers for instruction. Additional support services, such as special instructional periods and study-skills aid, are also being created. Much of this effort has grown out of a staff review of research literature on successful outcome-based education and a local plan for putting these ideas to work.

Clarkston High School. This school is in a small town in the southeastern corner of Washington. Its Communication, Curriculum, and Careers in the 21st Century Program has three interrelated components: (1) a sophisticated communication system that will place students and teachers in contact with information about schools, colleges, businesses, and individuals operating on the cutting edge of new developments in education; (2) a curriculum that will refocus subject matter, encourage teaching innovations, and apply relevant research; and (3) an intensive academic- and career-counseling component that starts in the freshman year. An essential part of the program is the intensive training of teachers to ensure that they are competent in new technology; effective in working with new teachers; and able to use information cooperatively with students, parents, and each other.

Bethel School District. This district, located near Tacoma, designed its Extended Learning Family Program to use the schools to break the cycles of abuse, teen pregnancy, welfare dependence, delinquency, truancy, and dropping out of school. This project builds upon and strengthens existing programs: district preschool, dropout prevention, alternative high school, adult mentors, and an independent community advisory board. New elements added include an elementary school for at-risk children and an evening/weekend school for working youth who have dropped out of the regular school system. Additional features include a four-day school week from September through July, weekly staff development programs, a guarantee to parents of student performance, individually structured learning programs, presence of adult learners in the school system, and using students to tutor other students. Evaluation, both by the community advisory board and by an independent evaluator, is a component of this program.

Others of the twenty-one schools plan to make new efforts to stress global education, some with a focus on the Pacific Rim; to renew efforts at multicultural education; and to improve coordination of school and social services to families at risk. All the schools and districts selected have multiple targets for improvement and commitment to continuous evaluation and modification of plans and activities.

One aspect of the process of application and selection that surprised all of us was the small number of requests for waivers from state rules, procedures, and regulations. There are three possible explanations for this: the laws and regulations may in fact not deter innovation; their full impact on constraining innovation cannot be anticipated this early in the developmental restructuring process; and teachers as well as the staff at the local level may not yet believe that rules and procedures really can be changed. We will see whether requests for waivers increase as these projects continue.

Washington's first Schools for the 21st Century began their new approach to education in August 1988. A Governor's Conference on Schools for the 21st Century, co-sponsored with the National Governors' Association, was held in October to bring people from the schools together and also to have them interact with nationally prominent educators. Opportunities of this kind should be frequent as we move along in this process because I believe that it will take time for educators and parents to realize the full implications of the freedom and opportunity that they have earned.

The Future

With no federal involvement—perhaps an unanticipated feature of the Reagan administration's reduction or elimination of federal education programs—and modest investments of new state resources, Washington State has taken some first steps in reforming and restructuring its schools. Some of the progress so far is admittedly symbolic, but the first steps have been taken toward change in the long run. Future activities related to the Schools for the 21st Century will be of three types:

• Continued support of the original twenty-one schools and districts and increasing the number of schools and districts involved.

• Analyzing all statutes and regulations governing education in the state, with an eye toward maximizing opportunities for innovation and accountability in schools at the local level.

• Initiating a new effort aimed at providing advanced technology to teachers and students.

The importance of our simultaneous efforts to restructure and improve schools and teacher education cannot be overemphasized. And our focus on improved student learning will require that we find new and better ways of assessing what students need to know, actually know, and can do. We are committed to achieving that goal.

A traditional approach to reform in the public sector has been to propose bold initiatives, with substantial new resources to support them. The reality of public leadership in the 1980s and, it appears, the 1990s, requires not less vision or creativity, but rather a different kind. Former ways of educating will have to be eased out by newer approaches. The budgetary restraints do not permit substantial add-ons. This means involving educators and parents, among others, in making hard choices and in restructuring operations.

The new role of governors in the educational environment is to solicit and provide momentum and limited resources to creative and energetic local approaches, to suggest new goals, to applaud the best efforts, and otherwise to get out of the way.

Governor Dick Thornburgh

★ Pennsylvania ★

Governor Thornburgh is currently U.S. attorney general with the Bush administration. He was the Republican governor of Pennsylvania from 1979 to 1987. While governor, he served as a member of the NGA Executive Committee and as chairman of the NGA Committee on Community and Economic Development.

The governor was educated at Yale University and University of Pittsburgh Law School. As an attorney, he has worked in the private sector with Aluminum Company of America and with a private law firm in Pittsburgh. His public sector experience prior to becoming governor included service as U.S. attorney for western Pennsylvania, and as assistant U.S. attorney general under President Ford.

His remarks as a gubernatorial fellow were made at Duke University on April 18, 1985.

★ ★ ★ ★ ★

The Three Mile Island Accident:
Its Lessons for Crisis Management

While serving as governor of Pennsylvania, I experienced an emergency management situation that no governor has faced before or since. The numerous lessons from that experience can be applied not only to the more familiar forms of emergencies, but also to the normal challenges of day-to-day governing.

Several things were on my mind at 7:50 on the morning of March 28, 1979. As a governor in office only seventy-two days, I was vitally interested in securing passage of my first budget, which would reflect my administration's priorities for the commonwealth. But, as I hosted a breakfast meeting for freshman Democratic legislators at my new official home in Harrisburg, several other matters also preoccupied me: the need to secure bipartisan support for a fiscal plan that reflected our campaign goals, stimulate economic development, provide better roads and schools, reform a costly welfare system, and crack down on violent crime as well as governmental corruption.

At 7:50 a.m., however, a telephone call from the state director of emergency management interrupted our meeting. An "accident" had occurred at the Three Mile Island nuclear power plant, located just ten miles downstream from the capital, in the middle of the Susquehanna River. The problem had actually begun at 4:00 in the morning, when vital cooling water started to escape through an open valve in the newest of two nuclear reactors at the plant. For the next two and a quarter hours, plant operators misread the symptoms, failed to close the valve, and mistakenly shut off an emergency cooling system that otherwise would have operated automatically. The reactor core overheated, and the worst accident in the history of commercial nuclear power was well underway.

That was back in 1979.

We now know that, though some of the reactor fuel heated to the point of melting, a disastrous "meltdown," as suggested in the popular movie "China Syndrome," would have been avoided. We now know that—though detectable amounts of radiation escaped into our air and water, and even into our milk, during the days of tension that were to follow—the amounts were limited and their impact on public health, if any, remains debatable. And we now know that a massive evacuation of the up to 200,000 people residing in the area, and its serious potential for panic, would have been far more dangerous and damaging than the accident itself.

But when I answered the phone at 7:50 on that March morning in 1979, we knew none of this. Nuclear power was still the technological marvel of our time—to some the ultimate answer to our growing energy problems, a source of electricity once described as "too cheap to meter"—and an industry whose safety record had been, or at least was thought to have been, second to none.

I had neither reason nor inclination to challenge these assumptions—except, perhaps, the one about my light bill being too cheap to meter. Nuclear jargon was a foreign language to me, and my exposure to emergency management at a nuclear power plant had been limited to a perfunctory briefing just after taking office. I knew enough, however, that the thought of issuing a general evacuation order first entered my mind at 7:50 that morning and never left me through the unprecedented days of decision making that followed.

Day One

On the first day, Wednesday, March 28, it was not yet clear that the governor personally would need to manage the civilian side of this crisis, but it was crystal clear that a new administration, which bore ultimate responsibility for public health and safety, had better start asking questions, analyzing the answers, and preparing for the worst. Because my staff and I were so unfamiliar with the existing state bureaucracy and because there simply was no state bureau of nuclear crisis management as such, let alone a precedent to study, we did something at the outset that was to serve us very well.

In lieu of the existing bureaucracy, I assembled what might be called an "ad hocracy": a team of close associates whose judgment and competence I could trust absolutely; and a support group of relevant state specialists whose capabilities were about to be tested under pressures none of them had ever known before. The "ad hocracy" included, among others:

• My lieutenant governor, who, in his additional roles as chairman of our Energy and Emergency Management Councils, would head our fact-finding effort during the early stages of the accident.

• My chief of staff, a former federal prosecutor whose instinct for asking the right questions of the right people at the right time served us admirably throughout the ordeal.

• My secretary of budget and administration, who would evaluate the state's existing emergency management apparatus, including evacuation plans, and find them deficient—a situation that we moved swiftly to correct.

• My director of communications, along with my principal speech-writing assistant, both of whom, as former reporters, shared an instinct for gathering and analyzing facts, as well as putting them in language the public could understand.

• And, of course, the specialists: the director of the Bureau of Radiation Protection, the secretaries of health and environmental resources, the director of emergency management, and various others who moved in and out of the group on an as-needed basis.

The "ad hocracy" reported to me only periodically at first, and those reports were sandwiched between other pressing, but somewhat normal, affairs of state. I believed it was important to conduct business as usual in the governor's office, and perhaps even more important to appear to be doing so. As the implications of the accident became more apparent, however, I began to cancel other appointments; and the "ad hocracy" virtually moved into my office for an extended, and unforgettable, stay.

Our first task was to find out exactly what was happening at the site of the accident. Trained both as an engineer and as a lawyer, I had a well-developed respect for the integrity of facts, and I instinctively demanded much more of my sources than opinion, conjecture, guesswork, or contradictory allegations. I wanted the facts as best they possibly could be determined and as quickly as they could possibly be assembled. In the case of Three Mile Island, this would prove to be far more difficult than any of us imagined.

The utility, its regulators, and other groups and institutions appeared to be contradicting each other, or telling the public either less than they knew or more than they knew. Self-appointed experts began to exaggerate either the danger or the safety of the situation. The credibility of the utility, which at first seemed to speak with many voices, and then with none at all, did not fare well—either with us, the media, or the public.

The company began that first day by seeking to minimize the accident—assuring us that "everything is under control," whereas we later learned that it was not; and that "all safety equipment functioned properly," though we later found that it did not. And, even when its technicians found that radiation levels in the area surrounding the island had climbed above normal, the company neglected to include that information in its statement to the public. The company had also vented radioactive steam into the air for about two and a half hours at midday, without informing the populace.

It fell to us, then, to tell the people of central Pennsylvania, as the lieutenant governor did at a 4:30 p.m. press conference, that "This situation is more complex than the company first led us to believe"; that radioactivity had indeed been released into the environment; that the company might make further discharges; and that we were "concerned" about all of this, but that off-site radioactivity levels had been decreasing during the afternoon and no evidence existed, as yet, that they ever had reached the danger point.

Although we continued, throughout the crisis, to monitor what utility officials were saying, we began to look elsewhere for sources of information who would be more credible to the public, as well as helpful to us. Among others, we turned inevitably to federal engineers and inspectors who had spent most of the first day inside the plant. Three of these on-site government experts briefed us that night and joined the lieutenant governor in a 10:00 p.m. press conference that was to end a long Day One for most members of the "ad hocracy."

I was an exception. My past reading habits would delay what otherwise might have been a deep, comfortable, and much-needed sleep because I recalled reading a book, reassuringly entitled *We Almost Lost Detroit*, an account by John G. Fuller of problems at the Enrico Fermi nuclear power plant in Michigan. I remembered Fuller's discussion of the consequences of core damage at the Michigan plant and realized that our federal experts had not raised this issue with respect to Three Mile Island during our evening briefing.

In 1979 few people realized there really was no danger of an actual nuclear explosion—mushroom cloud and all—from a nuclear power plant. That is not physically possible. The real catastrophe—as outlined by Fuller—would be the overheating of the reactor core to the point where it actually melts down and burns through its concrete and steel containment. The massive amounts of radioactive material that would be released could silently, but lethally, contaminate the environment for miles around and for centuries to come.

The term "China Syndrome" was derived, in fact, from the theory that such a core would be so hot that it could actually burn its way through to the other side of the earth. Ironically, the movie of that name was running in Harrisburg area theaters that very week, and its script incredibly described a meltdown as having the potential to contaminate an area "the size of the state of Pennsylvania."

I did manage to get to sleep that night, but it was not exactly easy, and I began Day Two with my new skepticism toward the experts and the industry fully intact.

Day Two

As the authors of a specially commissioned report were to write much later, the second day of the crisis was an "Interlude . . . a day for the drawing of deep breaths . . . a good time for members of Congress to put in an appearance," which, of course, they did.

Chairman Joseph Hendrie, of the Nuclear Regulatory Commission (NRC), meanwhile, was telling a congressional committee in Washington that we had been "nowhere near" a meltdown, though he had no way of really knowing this at the time. The company was holding its first full-fledged press conference since the accident and telling reporters that the plant was "stable" and that the controlled release of limited amounts of radioactivity into the atmosphere should soon be terminated. Those in charge seemed to feel that the worst of the accident had passed.

I wanted to believe that, of course, but I was not so sure. Company efforts to cool down the reactor were not working as well as expected, and self-appointed experts and eyewitnesses of dubious distinction continued to feed us unsubstantiated stories about dead animals, along with exaggerated warnings, various evacuation schemes, and a ridiculous tale—prompted by a poorly worded NRC press release in Washington—of radiation so powerful that it was penetrating four feet of concrete and spreading across the countryside up to sixteen miles from the plant. Signs were also popping up in grocery-store windows around the region proclaiming "We don't sell Pennsylvania milk."

Public faith in the experts and institutions was beginning to erode, and it was clear that the credibility of the governor's office was to become much more than simply a political asset for its occupant. That credibility was to become, perhaps, the last bulwark against a possible breakdown in civil authority and the chaos and panic such an occurrence would surely ignite.

Obviously, we were determined to preserve that bulwark. The time had come, I felt, for the state to become more visibly active and to use whatever credibility we had maintained to put things back into perspective—to inform the public that the situation was not as bad as some would have us fear, nor as good as others would have us believe.

Let me emphasize that we did not run to the capitol media center with every doomsday alarm, off-site rumor, pseudoscientific finding, or even credible piece of information that crossed my desk. We took our lumps from the media, in fact, for alleged "inaccessibility" because we spent hours and hours cross-checking one source against another and testing all our information for truth, accuracy, and significance. Once we did go public, even the grumpiest of reporters acknowledged that they did, indeed, come to depend on us for the truth about what was going on and what it all meant.

Although I did continue to seek advice and briefings from federal personnel working at the site, I sent our own state experts on radiation and nuclear engineering to the island to supplement and cross-check what we were being told. On their assurance that it was safe to do so, I also asked the lieutenant governor to go into the plant and bring back what was to become the first authentic layman's report on what it was like in there.

I wanted to know if the company technicians themselves were in a panic, and his later description of the workers as calm and cool was reassuring, to say the least. The mere fact that the lieutenant governor had actually gone inside the plant at that particular time was perhaps even more reassuring to a citizenry bombarded by the various "Chicken Littles" in our midst. Finally, we all agreed, it was time for me to become publicly involved in the effort.

A governor cannot command the television cameras free of editing the way a president of the United States can. Yet I felt a need that afternoon to communicate directly with those who had been living with the uncertainties of this strange and unprecedented event. And so, opening my first press conference since the accident began, I addressed my remarks directly to the citizens.

"There is no cause for alarm," I said, "nor any reason to disrupt your daily routine, nor any reason to feel that public health has been affected by the events on Three Mile Island. This applies to pregnant women, this applies to small children, and this applies to our food supplies. . . . While we believe the danger is under control at this time, we recognize that it is very important that all of us remain alert and informed. We will . . . do so."

My briefing to the press that day was followed by a statement from one of the experts from the NRC, who declared, to my astonishment, that "the danger is over." I learned later that night that another on-site expert privately disagreed, and that water samples indicated that the "core damage is very bad."

Although Thursday ended on this somewhat edgy note, it was a mere prelude to a Friday I will never forget.

Day Three

Day three was to become known as the day of the great evacuation scare—the day that illustrated not only the folly, but also the very real danger, of trying to manage this kind of an emergency by long distance. It began, once again, in the early morning hours, when the shift operators at Three Mile Island were alarmed by a buildup of steam pressure on a valve. Without approval from anybody, they simply opened it and allowed the steam, along with a substantial amount of radioactive material, to escape into the atmosphere.

Helicopter readings, taken directly above the plant's exhaust stack, indicated a radiation exposure rate of 1,200 millirems per hour—a rate certainly high enough to warrant an evacuation, if the readings had been taken in nearby Middletown, in Harrisburg, or anywhere away from the plant site itself. But, coming directly out of the stack, where the materials immediately were dispersed, such a reading was no more significant than those taken during the previous two days of the crisis.

Unfortunately, in a classic manifestation of what I was later to call the "garble gap" between Harrisburg and Washington, the NRC's Washington-based Executive Management Team thought that the readings had, indeed, been taken in an off-site area and decided to recommend that we evacuate all residents within a five-mile radius of the plant.

Also unfortunately, this Washington group forwarded its recommendation up to us through our emergency management director instead of our radiation protection director, who could have corrected the error and spared central Pennsylvania from reaching the very brink of panic. And, even more unfortunately, the emergency management director called a local civil defense director, who informed a local radio station that an evacuation order from me might well be imminent. I had yet to be so informed.

When the word finally did reach me that a "Doc Collins" from Washington was saying we should evacuate, I had no idea who he was or by what authority or for what reason he was making such a recommendation— and I did not intend to evacuate thousands of people on such incomplete information. For, no matter how well they are planned, massive evacuations can kill and injure people—especially the aged and infirm, infants in incubators, other hospital patients, and even the able-bodied bystander who—like the usher at the exit of a burning theater—happens to be in the wrong place at the wrong time.

So I started asking questions, and my difficulty in obtaining answers was compounded by the jamming of our switchboard—thanks not only to the premature disclosure of an erroneous evacuation advisory, but also the mysterious tripping of an emergency siren that soon had hearts pounding and eyes widening all over the city. People were throwing their belongings into trucks and cars, locking up their shops and homes, and packing to get out of town. If ever we were close to a general panic, this was the moment.

I placed a call to the NRC chairman himself, and, by the time I reached him, his staff had discovered what my own radiation experts were telling me: that the evacuation advisory was a mistake. The NRC group withdrew that advisory, and I immediately went on the air to assure our people that the alarm was a false one and that no general evacuation would occur.

Shortly after that, I was on the phone with President Carter. Our two staffs had put aside partisan interests in dealing with this crisis from the beginning, and rightly so. They had established the kind of "friendship under fire" such incidents frequently create. My conversation with the president was therefore honest, open, direct, and, above all, productive. I asked for, and Carter agreed to send us, a high-ranking professional who would proceed to Three Mile Island as his personal representative. This expert would merge solid technical and management expertise with an on-site perspective, and report accurately and directly to the White House, to me, and to the people on what was going on out there, what was not going on, and why.

Harold Denton, the NRC's director of nuclear reactor regulation, turned out to be the perfect choice, and his arrival later in the day would represent a turning point in the crisis. For the moment, however, the evacuation question was not entirely settled. Although relieved that a general evacuation was unnecessary, we were deeply troubled by the confusion that episode exposed in Washington, as well as in the plant, and by the uncertainty over what might happen next.

We began to wonder on our own if pregnant women and small children— those residents most vulnerable to the effects of radiation, yet relatively easy to move—should be encouraged to leave the area nearest the plant. We decided to put that question directly to Chairman Hendrie, who answered: "If my wife were pregnant and had small children in the area, I would get them out, because we don't know what is going to happen."

Shortly after noon on Day Three of the crisis, therefore, I recommended that pregnant women and preschoolers leave the area within five miles of the plant until further notice, and that all schools within that zone be closed as well. I also ordered the opening of evacuation centers at various sites outside the area to shelter those who had no place to go. "Current readings," I told the people, "are no higher than they were yesterday but the continued presence of radioactivity in the area and the possibility of further emissions lead me to exercise the utmost of caution."

Denton arrived at the plant that afternoon. A three-way hot line was installed there to connect him with me and with the president. Later that night, Denton and I met for the first time and spent an hour and a half reviewing the situation. It was quite clear that his slow and relaxed North Carolina drawl, his way of smiling naturally as he spoke, his ease and apparent candor with the press, his ability to speak plain English as well as nuclear jargon—all these factors were soon to make him the world's most believable expert on the technical situation at Three Mile Island. And his value would soon be put to the test.

While he was on his way up to Pennsylvania, his colleagues in Washington finally referred publicly to the theoretical possibility of a meltdown, in an accurate but poorly handled statement which caused even that most credible of all Americans, Walter Cronkite, to open the CBS Evening News by saying, "We are faced with the remote but very real possibility of a nuclear meltdown at the Three Mile Island atomic power plant."

Denton joined me in a press conference that night, put the facts in perspective, lowered the level of concern, and earned his spurs with the press—and with me. Although we did continue to cross-check his observations against those of my own team, we quickly became convinced that he was as credible as he appeared to be.

As Day Three wound down, I felt we finally were equipped to handle the misstatements, second-guessing, and false alarms that were certain to continue.

Day Four

Harold Denton's long series of regular press briefings in Middletown, near the plant site, began on Day Four, Saturday, March 31. They did serve to keep things relatively calm, and I felt it safe to leave Harrisburg for the first time since the accident. I wanted to visit some of the people who had spent the night—at my advice—on cots and blankets covering the floor of a sports arena in nearby Hershey. As I walked through what amounted to an indoor campground, I was met by the anxious faces of young mothers and mothers-to-be and the tired eyes of children who had fallen way behind in their sleep. Giving them a brief pep talk over a shaky public address system, I thanked them for their confidence, their cooperation, and their bravery.

It was there that I resolved to do all that I could, for the remainder of my term, to see that neither human nor technological error on Three Mile Island would ever be allowed to threaten these people again—a commitment that was to consume an inordinate amount of my time, even to this very day.

As for March 31, 1979, however, human and technological errors were to provide yet one more scare for these good people. Based on information given to it by an anonymous NRC source in Washington, a wire service ran a news bulletin that night that read: "U-R-G-E-N-T- . . . The NRC now says the gas bubble atop the nuclear reactor at Three Mile Island shows signs of becoming potentially explosive." This fear was totally groundless. The hydrogen bubble would never explode in the reactor vessel. As one review of the crisis later recalled: "It would blow up, instead, in the media."

The bulletin, in its most cryptic and chilling form, moved like a hurricane advisory across the bottoms of prime-time television screens everywhere that Saturday night. In Harrisburg, people streamed out of downtown bars and restaurants. Our switchboard jammed again, and a herd of reporters stampeded into my press office—not for the story itself, but demanding to know if they should get out of town.

Obviously, we had to move fast. We called Denton at the plant and learned that there was no danger of an imminent explosion and no cause for alarm. My press secretary, skipping our normal clearance procedures, banged out a three-paragraph statement to that effect and literally ran it down to the capitol newsroom. Concurrently, we asked Denton, who was on his way to my office, to go directly to the newsroom instead—which he did. Within minutes, stories quoting our statement, and then Denton's impromptu news conference, began to move on the wires, and another potential panic seemed to have been avoided.

In the course of this "bubble" drill, we had been in touch with the White House and discussed the possibility of a visit to the area by the president himself. Press Secretary Jody Powell authorized me to announce that Carter would, indeed, be joining us in the near future, and I did. Powell issued a similar advisory out of Washington. That was to be, in effect, the end of the panic-avoidance phase of our crisis.

Day Five

The president arrived the very next day, and he and I toured the plant together—in full view of network television cameras. The image that was beamed around the world on April 1, Day Five of the crisis, had its desired effect. If it was safe enough at Three Mile Island for the governor of Pennsylvania and the president of the United States, it had to be safe enough for anyone.

Over the next several days, Denton continued to oversee the cooling down of the reactor core and to offer progress reports to a press contingent that was fast losing interest in the story. On April 6, just ten days after that fateful opening of what had become the most famous power plant valve in the world, I prepared to tell our people that the crisis had passed, and that those who had chosen to leave the area could, indeed, "come home again."

The Managerial Lessons

Although I recognize that no other governor has ever faced a nuclear emergency, and though I pray that none ever will again, the experience suggests a number of lessons that could be useful to other state executives, not only in managing such unforeseen crises, but also in handling some of the normal problems of governing as well.

1. Perhaps the first among these lessons is to "expect the unexpected" and be prepared to adjust accordingly. For us, if it was not Three Mile Island, it was three-mile gas lines; if not a water shortage, a flood; if not a transit strike, a subway crash; if not an underground mine fire, a prison hostage crisis. The importance of limiting those things that any governor should attempt to do in the time allowed, the careful choice of battles to

be waged, is implicit in the fact that some of the toughest of them are chosen for us. Upon taking office, any governor should make sure not only that the state's existing emergency apparatus is adequate, but also that good men and women are in place to handle the administration's planned agenda as well—should the chief executive become occupied by an event that was never planned at all.

2. When an emergency does strike, a trusted "ad hocracy" may be far more useful than an entrenched or untested bureaucracy. It was not in our job descriptions to function like a virtual grand jury, grilling witnesses to a nuclear emergency, and then to serve as a communications center for the people—but it worked. A chief executive should not be afraid to scramble the organization chart—as we did during the Three Mile Island crisis, or in perhaps a more familiar example, as President Kennedy did during the Cuban missile crisis, when his own brother's advice weighed more heavily with him than did that of the secretary of state or his military experts.

3. Be ready to restrain those who, as described by our emergency management director during the crisis, may be "leaning forward in the trenches," helmets, sirens, and all, and thinking solely in terms of "doing something," regardless of the safety or necessity. This applies not only to emergency volunteers and staff, and not only to emergencies, but also to bureaucrats, technocrats, academicians, medical and other professionals, and, yes, even to colleagues in politics as well. The impulse in government to act merely for the sake of action, or to test a plan or agency simply because it is there, must be kept firmly under control.

4. Be wary of what might be called "emergency macho"—the temptation to stay up all night and then brag about it. Although it is often important for the governor to maintain a visible and reassuring presence, anyone making life or death decisions for thousands of innocent people owes them a mind that is clear and a body that is rested.

5. Do not try to manage an emergency from anywhere but the site itself. This does not mean that the governor must be on-site personally, but someone must be in charge there whose competence and judgment the governor can trust. Most of our communications problems originated in Washington. Even Harold Denton, I later learned, had been a major participant in that bogus evacuation advisory the NRC sent up to us on the third day. He later was to concede that "I've learned that emergencies can only be managed by people at the site. They can't be managed back in Washington."

6. Search for and evaluate the facts and their sources again and again, and communicate those facts truthfully and carefully to the people, remembering that credibility can be as fragile as it is crucial during the heat of a genuine public emergency.

7. Respect, but do not depend on, the news media. Throughout the Three Mile Island incident, we developed a considerable empathy for the more than four hundred reporters from around the world who were assigned to cover the event. Their frustrations mirrored ours in the attempt to establish reliable facts. In many instances, our decision makers and the members of the media "compared notes" on vital issues to ensure both the quality of the reporting and the quality of action within state government. Not all the reporting was reliable, however, and some was downright outrageous. For example, I was informed that a British news organ, in its attempt to convey the gravity of the situation, carried an item to the effect that "the governor's wife, pregnant with their first child, has left the area." In fact, my wife was not pregnant; we already had four children, and, most important, she stayed with me in Harrisburg during the entire episode, as did the lieutenant governor, incidentally, whose wife was pregnant with their very first child, and who also stayed with him.

8. Forget partisanship, for there is no Republican or Democratic way to manage a real emergency. In our stewardship of this most basic of all public trusts, we inevitably survive or suffer together, and, not incidentally, so do the people we are elected to serve.

9. Value and learn from history. Although the Fuller book on the Fermi plant proved useful, let me assure you that, if one of my colleagues had already experienced a nuclear emergency like Three Mile Island and had recounted it in book form, such a publication would not long have lingered on my shelf.

10. And, finally, as that well-known American "philosopher," baseball player Yogi Berra, once said: "It ain't over till it's over."

The Aftermath

The year after the accident, I had to step into a new furor over a plan to vent radioactive krypton gas into the atmosphere as part of the Three Mile Island cleanup operation. Public hearings on the safety of the plan almost turned into riots. One imaginative opponent of the venting put on a Superman suit and proceeded to "choke" himself on the front steps of the capitol. I took the unorthodox step of asking the Union of Concerned Scientists, a well-known group of nuclear industry critics, to study the venting plan. When they concluded that it posed no physical threat to public health and safety, the venting proceeded peacefully.

The year after that, however, we learned that no plan had been devised to fund the billion-dollar effort necessary to decontaminate the damaged reactor. Because the site cannot be considered truly safe until that cleanup has been completed, and because the established institutions were at an impasse, I had no choice but to develop and push a national cost-sharing plan for its funding. Although some of the subsequent funding commitments may not be as firm as I would prefer at this point, the plan does seem to be working.

These lessons—along with other byproducts of the Three Mile Island experience—helped us to reach most of the other goals we had established for Pennsylvania that were so rudely interrupted on that fateful day in 1979. Thanks to this "shakedown cruise," we learned, for example, whom we could depend on to do good work under pressure in state government, and we did so in perhaps a tenth of the time taken by most new administrations. These people were to continue to serve Pennsylvania with distinction as we passed our budgets, cleaned up corruption, reduced crime, expanded economic opportunities, reformed our welfare and education systems, and began to rebuild our roads and bridges. Obviously, we were also reelected.

Even today, however, the cooling towers of Three Mile Island continue to represent a greater demand on my time than I ever imagined possible. In the immediate aftermath of the accident, we were engaged in hearings over the company's effort to restart the undamaged Unit 1 reactor there, a facility that had been shut down for refueling at the time of the accident, less than 200 yards away, at Unit 2. Unit 1 has been out of service ever since, and I maintain that it should remain so until all questions of health and safety—including the competence and integrity of company management—have been successfully addressed and resolved by the NRC.

I am not now, and never have been, an ideological opponent of commercial nuclear power. To me, that would be like opposing the use of the automobile because God didn't mean for us to drive, or the airplane because God didn't mean for us to fly. No, I believe that commercial nuclear power can and ought to reclaim a positive role in our society. But I also contend that, before this is possible, before the debate over the future of this awesome technology can be moved off dead center, the industry and the government have a solemn obligation to acknowledge that the accident at Three Mile Island should never have happened in America, and to assure us that it will never be allowed to happen again.

Governor Terry E. Branstad
★ Iowa ★

Governor Branstad has been the Republican governor of Iowa since 1983. He was chairman of NGA in 1989-90 and has chaired the NGA Committee on Agriculture and the Task Force on Rural Development.

The governor has served in the U.S. Army, worked as an attorney with Branstad and Schwarm, and was Iowa's lieutenant governor. He maintains an active interest in the Branstad family farming operation. Governor Branstad graduated from the University of Iowa and Drake University Law School.

His remarks as a gubernatorial fellow were made at Duke University on November 4, 1987.

★ ★ ★ ★ ★

Restructuring and Downsizing
the Iowa State Government

Of all my accomplishments as governor of Iowa, the one I am most proud of is the major reorganization and downsizing of the state government. In fact, it was praised in the *Journal of State Government.*

Reorganization in government has a bad name. Some pundits like to say that when you do not know what else to do in government, you ought to reorganize. In Iowa, the same attitude prevailed in some quarters. Indeed, when I first examined the idea of reorganizing the state government, I noticed that the whole issue was controversial. For example, one of my political opponents called it "rearranging the chairs on the deck of the Titanic." But despite that kind of negativism and skepticism, we made major strides.

Although I was a first-term governor, who was engaged in a close battle for reelection during the depths of the worst farm crisis since the Depression, I proposed the most sweeping reorganization in the history of the state government, tangled with every interest group imaginable, worked with a legislature overwhelmingly controlled by the opposition party, and obtained passage of 90 percent of the reorganization package.

The Need for Action

The reasons for the restructuring of government in Iowa were similar to the need for reorganization elsewhere. Organizations often reflect the problems of the past, not the opportunities of the future. Iowa is a medium-sized state whose political tradition is moderately conservative. At the same time, it prides itself on its relatively progressive response to solving problems. As a result, when problems have been discovered, since 1846, the state government has often been called on to solve them. A program was then created and an agency was established to run it, but once the problem had been solved, the agency remained and found a new mission for itself.

A good example of this was the Energy Policy Council. It had been founded in the early seventies during the first Arab oil embargo. Farmers and others in Iowa were experiencing difficulty in obtaining desperately needed oil supplies, so the council was formed to help set up a priority system of oil allocation in the state. We led the nation in terms of responding to this problem, and the federal government copied our system. But by 1985, we had surplus oil supplies, prices were at several-year lows, and it was easy for people to obtain oil to fuel their tractors and cars. Yet the budget of the Energy Policy Council was three times the size of its original one. In fact, the council set about finding new missions for itself, including reporting on changes in gasoline prices, a service that was already being provided by the American Automobile Association.

In short, over the years government tends to grow unwieldy, and it did so in Iowa. Our history of responding to perceived problems left us with 68 departments and 190 boards and commissions. My span of control was 1:250. The result was extreme difficulty in setting priorities in government. Because of the large number of entities competing for limited funds, the response was to spread the resources widely and thinly. The effect was increasing mediocrity in the quality of government services, excessive costs, and a reduced ability by leaders to direct the course of the state's future.

In addition, Iowa faced an economic crisis in the 1980s, and this helped condition the need to reorganize the government. In 1979, interest rates began rising to all-time highs, and the dollar shot up in value in relation to other currencies. Also, President Carter imposed an embargo on grain sales to the Soviet Union. The result was seven straight years of budget problems in the state. My predecessor, Robert Ray, made two across-the-board cuts, and I did likewise. A general sales-tax increase was needed to meet our minimum obligations in 1983, and we had a budget deficit of close to $200 million. Yet despite the sales-tax increase and across-the-board cuts, the fiscal problems remained. In early 1985, as I reviewed the budget, I found that I had to cut across the board by an additional 3.85 percent—the largest cut made in Iowa until that time. And despite that, another $60 million was needed to make sure that the budget was balanced for the next year.

Those severe budgetary problems made it clear to me that we could not continue to simply make further across-the-board cuts and lower the tide of mediocrity in governmental services. We simply had to set priorities and change the way we did things. Fortunately, public expectations of the need to reorganize and downsize government were strong.

Three separate so-called "economy reports" had been prepared for the state during the past decade and a half. Two governors' economy committee reports, in 1969 and 1979, had recommended a vast reorganization of the government and creation of a cabinet form of government. However, neither of these recommendations were significantly carried out. These reports, prepared by an outside group of business experts, never met the test of political reality.

In 1983, during my first year in office, I commissioned an economy and efficiency effort from the inside of government—utilizing its personnel to recommend ways in which the structure and operation of government could be changed to make it more efficient. We acted on many of these recommendations, but the savings were not large.

In short, most of the past reorganization and downsizing plans either had not been recommended or had not been accomplished. There was a growing sense that government was the only part of the Iowa economy that continued to grow; that though many families had to tighten their belts, government was not doing likewise. As a result of the unwieldy governmental structure, the continuing economic problems in the state, and public expectations of reduction in the size of government, in June 1985 I met with key department heads and the leaders of the past economic studies and sold them on the idea that the time was right to effect a major restructuring and downsizing of the state government.

In September of that year, I imposed the largest across-the-board cut ever made in Iowa, and I also announced something new. I indicated that I would no longer impose any more of these kinds of cuts because they failed to recognize the need for fresh priorities in order to deal with the new economic realities of the day. I also indicated that I would retain a consultant and provide recommendations for a restructuring and downsizing of government that I would recommend to the legislators in December for consideration in their January session. January also began an election year, in which I was engaged in a tough battle for reelection, during which I would be proven to be either a savvy risk-taker or a reckless political leader. Fortunately, the voters decided I was the former.

Nature of the Process

I am particularly proud of the methodology we used in formulating the restructuring and downsizing proposal. I believe it could well serve as a model for other state government organizations that are seeking to change their structure and focus. The key elements of that methodology were as follows. First, we used what I call both the "inside" and "outside" models in an attempt to create a synergy that would give us a realistic as well as bold plan.

Many governmental reorganization efforts presume that government should be run like a business and that a clean and crisp organizational chart indicating clear lines of authority and eliminating all duplications is needed. This "outside" model utilizes business executives to come in and redraw government lines. The problem is that government is not a business. It has a constituent-service, not a profit, motive. As a result, these outside model plans are often bold, but politically unrealistic, and consequently are never carried out.

The "inside" model, which seeks to avoid political mistakes, utilizes groups within government that know its realities to recommend ways in which services and programs can be revamped. The problem with this approach is that it often avoids political mistakes, but considerable back-scratching ensues and little of significance is recommended.

I believed that we needed to have a combination of both: a strong outside group that would recommend bold changes and a group of inside "hotshots" who could provide a sense of political realism. The resulting synergy helped us to formulate a viable plan that had a decent chance of passage.

Second, we studied both the organization of government and its programs and used separate processes to handle each with regard to the reorganization. Our consultants as well as top government and business leaders reviewed the existing organizational structure, which was in sad disarray. We looked for ways to group like functions and at the same time to reduce duplicate administrative costs. Separately, we worked with department heads, who put together a reverse ranking of the programs they administered, indicating those of lowest priority first. We then used that mechanism to identify programs that could be eliminated or downsized. Most departments provided accurate information and helped avoid political pitfalls.

Third, we used both a "top-down" and a "bottom-up" process. We interviewed each of the department heads and their key subordinates to ascertain their ideas on the reorganization. This gave us so-called "bottom-up" information. At the same time, a steering committee of two of the strongest department heads and some of the key business leaders was organized to work with consultants and my staff to develop the "top-down" approach on the best way to reshape the government. We allowed the top to meet the bottom, and the result was a mix of both the strong and the sensible.

Fourth, we decided to create the reorganization plan quickly and to carry it out immediately instead of waiting for years to make the recommendations and to put them into effect. We gave the consultants three months to formulate the recommendations, and we decided to act on every administrative one immediately and to effect the legislative changes at the beginning of the next fiscal year. In fact, we rewrote the entire budget request based upon the newly proposed organization. This compression of time allowed us to build enough momentum to reduce the drag caused by the opposing interest groups during this entire process. If we had waited longer to devise or to accomplish the plan, the interest groups would likely have simply picked it apart.

Fifth, we hired an outside consultant to help coordinate the report. We used the Government Services Section of the Peat, Marwick, Mitchell company because it was knowledgeable and creditable. Employing a consultant firm of this high caliber bolsters a state's reorganization efforts because it allows the firm to be the lightning rod for controversial items while, at the same time, lending an aura of creditability to the entire project. This was particularly useful to us as we fought legislative battles.

Sixth, we brought the legislative leaders into the process. They were given special briefings while we formulated the project, and we listened to their advice and suggestions. We also worked closely with the leading media in the state, giving them advance information about our efforts. In response, they ran a series of stories that gave examples of why the state government had grown excessively and needed to be cut back.

Seventh, we emphasized implementation through the entire report. Past reports and past efforts to reorganize government focused on an attempt to devise a workable plan. We spent just as much energy and time in producing a scheme for putting it into effect. We appointed a director of restructuring within our new Department of Management, and that individual served as a ramrod for the entire effort.

Eighth, we decided to create no new levels of administration. One of the problems of reorganization proposals is that they often do so. Thus, those people who wish to see the size of government cut point out that reorganizations often result in additions to the bureaucracy, not subtractions, and a natural constituency for reorganization evaporates. Therefore, we decided not to establish a cabinet form of government, but instead created only enough agencies to allow us to have better coordinated control of state government, but not so many as to create a new layer of administration.

Ninth, we decided to group the departments into clusters reflecting the major issues facing the state. We formed six separate clusters of agencies focusing on education, economic development, human services, administration and control, public safety, and infrastructure. Logical development of the agency clusters along the lines of major issues facing the state was well accepted by its leaders and gave us coordinating ability without excessive administration.

Tenth, we maintained some citizen involvement in the policy development for and oversight of state agencies, but we removed the myriad of advisory commissions and boards from the day-to-day management of the government. Over the years, many boards and commissions not only gained the authority to appoint the major department heads, but also had the ability to manage the day-to-day operations of government. That left me with a very difficult situation: I was responsible for the management of state government, but in many cases I had no authority to do so. Therefore, while maintaining many of these advisory groups, we also made them just that: groups designed to provide public oversight and input into state agencies, but not to run them.

Eleventh, we decided to reduce the span of control. A 1:250 span is simply impossible for any manager, whatever his or her abilities. Instead of establishing a number of departments or a cabinet, we simply created twenty reasonably sized agencies that could report directly to the governor without creating a new ladder of administrative control.

Twelfth, we established a framework that will offer opportunities for further consolidation of state government. This is particularly true in so-called "umbrella" departments. Because they were first placed under one roof with little integration, we gained future opportunities for further consolidation and downsizing.

Thirteenth, our plan gave the governor authority to run the government. The leaders of many significant departments such as transportation, natural resources, and education had been appointed by commissions rather than by the governor. As the result, in the major policy areas he had no day-to-day line authority over those departments. In establishing that authority, we won serious battles with many people and organizations, including those in the educational community.

Fourteenth, we expanded our ability to control state budgets, programs, and policy and planning development. In the past, the budget control mechanism in the comptroller's office had handled only the budget formulation process. Policy development was scattered throughout all the agencies, and the planning function had been bogged down with program administration. We transferred all budget, program, and policy and planning development processes into a new Department of Management and structured it to parallel the clusters of agencies that had been created.

We hired top state government professionals to head each of these clusters and gave them wide authority to develop budgets, make long-range plans, and operate the policy development process. We also established a central responsibility within the Department of Management to stimulate further economies and efficiencies in the various departments. This ongoing mechanism helped to carry out the program quickly and assisted in identifying future savings in the post-reorganization era.

Fifteenth, we combined many like functions to cut administrative costs. The extent of our success in this endeavor was amazing. For example, in the personnel area alone, we cut out more than $4 million by eliminating duplicate personnel administration that had been scattered throughout the departments. Similar results were obtained in the accounting, hearing officer, licensing, and audit function areas. Interestingly, because of our consolidation and coordination of the personnel functions, the American Federation of State, County, and Municipal Employees supported our efforts inasmuch as uniform application of personnel policies in the state also benefited its members.

Sixteenth, we eliminated duplicate, obsolete, and unnecessary programs. Those like the fuel allocation programs that were still in operation and yet were designed to serve another era were eliminated. Other programs, like the state's control of retail sale of liquor, were privatized; and duplicate payments that were being made to school districts for the same students were discontinued.

Seventeenth, and most important, the entire process was budget-driven. We made it clear that this was just not reorganization for reorganization's sake. It was imperative in order to save $40 million in state operating costs. Otherwise, we noted, either taxes would have to be raised or further across-the-board cuts would need to be made.

Using the foregoing principles, then, on December 3, 1985, I announced the massive reorganization proposal for state government. I proposed a reduction in the number of agencies from sixty-eight to eighteen and created six cluster groups. All department heads would be appointed by the governor, but control of the budget, policy, and planning of state government would be centralized. We proposed to cut $40 million of operating costs out of state government, and we wrote the budget to reflect it. We examined a hundred different recommendations to reduce or eliminate programs.

But it is also important to recognize what was not in the report. It dealt only with that portion of state government that is generally under the governor's control. Local governments and the regent-directed educational institutions were not part of the reorganization process, and we did not attempt to impose a structure on them. Instead, they were given incentives to restructure and downsize their own operations. For example, we encouraged local school districts to consolidate by providing property tax incentives to do so and by furnishing other incentives for the sharing of superintendents. Subsequently, almost a hundred school districts in the state took part in that sharing program. We gave the board of regents a mandate to accomplish their own organizational audit and to focus on their existing structure and programs in the same way we had. And I promised that they could keep whatever money they saved.

The process of obtaining legislative approval for this major effort was difficult, to say the least. The legislature was controlled by members of the opposition party. And in January we were entering an election year in which the former majority leader of the senate was challenging me for governor. Our biggest problem was in attempting to overcome what I call the "LCD" (lowest common denominator) factor. Oftentimes, the legislature will end up able to pass only the lowest common denominator, which is, in effect, determined by what interest groups want. In this case, if those groups were to prevail, we would end up with little or no change. We had to overcome the "LCD" factor.

We wrote a 500-page bill to establish the program, and our restructuring director worked closely with the legislators throughout the process. In effect, we tied the legislature in knots by totally dominating the agenda and by creating substantial budget and public momentum.

The Results

As a result, we accomplished 90 percent of what we set out to do:

• We reduced the number of departments from sixty-eight to twenty.

• We eliminated about forty boards and commissions.

• We cut not $40 million but $60 million out of the state's operating budget.

• We created a Department of Management that had authority over the budget as well as policy and planning.

• We gave the governor the authority to appoint all department heads.

• We slashed the staff by more than 1,700 individuals—10 percent of the central state government—but only seven layoffs were necessary.

• We established an early retirement program to ease two hundred people out of state government positions.

• We eliminated one hundred positions that had been vacant but for which funding had been provided.

• We created a performance evaluation and objectives process in which the governor meets with every department head each month to review the extent to which he or she is meeting previously agreed upon objectives.

• We established a Department of Personnel to control personnel and benefit functions.

• We became the only state in the nation's history to privatize its entire retail liquor operations without breaking the state's budget.

• We created a budget process that allowed us to meet our priority-driven goals of economic development and education. I was able to recommend a budget that substantially increased funding for education and economic development while reducing administrative costs in state government by 8.4 percent.

In short, Iowa was far leaner, more focused, and better directed: our effort was a tremendous success. We accomplished the most significant restructuring and downsizing of government in the state's history. We had, in effect, cleaned up the organizational structure and made the government more accountable and effective. Most important, we allowed it to be priority-driven. Given the series of economic problems we faced in the state, it was essential that the government be able to direct and lead the economic revitalization that was necessary. The new structure made it possible for us to do just that.

The Lessons

Various key lessons resulted from this effort.

First, whenever you want to reorganize, don't call the plan "reorganization." That term implies rearrangement, not redirection. Find another term like "restructuring" or "downsizing" to describe your efforts.

Second, make the process to restructure government budget-driven. Stress that this is needed for the state to reach its goals to avoid tax increases and to be able to set priorities to achieve major goals. In short, make people feel like they are going to receive benefits from this effort, not just keep losing them.

Third, do it quickly. Do not let interest groups peck your plan to death. Move rapidly and efficiently.

Fourth, involve as many key people as possible in the development of your plan in a controlled setting. Two of our strongest department heads were intimately associated with the plan, as were major business leaders. We also obtained commitments from legislative leaders early in the policy development process and gave them an opportunity to provide input. We also informed the media as we established the policy initiatives so they had good knowledge of the plan.

Fifth, use outside assistance. The day-to-day management problems of state government often result in overburdening of the staff and preclude focus on the long term or the grand scheme. An outside consultant helped us concentrate on the big picture and also lent an aura of creditability to the project.

Sixth, be humane about your effort. If people think you are cruel and heartless in your reorganization of government, they will not support it. But if you provide a cushion for them to withdraw from the system and if you treat them fairly, it can be accomplished. No lawsuits were initiated by any state employee even though we reduced the total size of the government by 10 percent and eliminated 1,700 positions from the payroll.

Seventh, build up a general constituency to counter interest group opposition. We established a public relations plan to garner public support, which we fostered and responded to. Work with the media to gain the backing of the people, and obtain early commitment from legislative leaders to withstand pressures from outside forces.

Eighth, market your plan. We used charts to show the "before and after" of state government and documented how Iowans were going to receive better service and avoid tax increases. This kind of aggressive marketing plan was the key to selling the people and the legislators on the reorganization.

Other Ramifications

In November 1986, eleven months after I outlined the massive restructuring and downsizing program, I was elected to a second term as my state's governor. I then presided over a dramatically reorganized government, one that provided a much better ability to manage and control state government. But to retain these gains, vigilance had to be maintained.

Interest groups that failed to achieve their goals during the restructuring debate began attempting to influence portions of the restructured government during the ensuing legislative sessions. Divisions were trying to become departments again, and new entities sought to be created. Only the governor could stand strong and fend off these efforts.

In addition, the legislature discovered that the governor acquired a significant additional degree of control over the management of state government. As a result, the legislators have engaged in much stricter review of the department heads during the confirmation process. One amendment added during the reorganizational debate required that all department heads be approved by two-thirds of the senate every four years. Therefore, these appointments must be carefully made.

Using the new organization to deliver on the promises we made when we started reorganization, we cut $60 million out of the operational budgets of state government. We delivered a priority-driven budget that was focused on economic development and education. And we avoided general tax increases as the result, in part, of restructuring and downsizing.

We also used the new structure to enhance efficiency. I established a series of monthly progress review sessions with department heads. I worked with them to establish their budgets and identify programmatic and affirmative action targets. This provided department heads with substantial flexibility while making certain that my goals were being met.

Then too, I began using the new organization to root out further inefficiencies in government and to accomplish some of the unfinished business of reorganization. Because we discovered that a number of individuals and sections of state government were rendered, to some extent, dysfunctional by the reorganized government, we established a second phase of the reorganization process that set up a special personnel class to assist those individuals. Plans were made to create an outplacement and early retirement program to help move them out of their current positions in a humane way.

In addition, we began using the new structure to review the way state government delivers services locally. A special task force identified enormous duplication of effort in this area, especially in hearing officer, enforcement, auditing, and investigation functions. Also, I asked all departments to present plans to me to establish a single set of geographical service areas for all their programs. This was necessary because some departments had dozens of different service delivery configurations. I believe that the coordination of service delivery within the departments and across departmental lines can produce substantial savings through co-location, coordination of functions, and reduction of staff.

Finally, I used the reorganization effort to maintain pressure on other entities of government to do the same. We continued to provide incentives for local governmental units to review their operations, sharpen their efficiency, and reorganize where savings could be achieved. And the regents undertook a comprehensive organizational audit of their entire operations with the goal of refocusing their efforts into areas of priority.

In summary, the restructuring and downsizing of government in Iowa was not the end, but the beginning. It was the beginning of a better focused, directed, and controlled state government. It was also the beginning of an effort to bolster the economic revitalization of our state.

Governor Richard D. Lamm
★ Colorado ★

Governor Lamm is currently director of the Center for Public Policy and Contemporary Issues in Denver, Colorado. He was the Democratic governor of Colorado from 1975 to 1987, and chaired the NGA Committee on Human Resources and the Task Force on Tax Reform.

The governor's career has included positions as a certified public accountant, an attorney, and a law professor. He also served as a member of the state legislature. Governor Lamm graduated from the University of Wisconsin and earned a law degree from the University of California.

His remarks as a gubernatorial fellow were made at Duke University on March 27, 1986.

★ ★ ★ ★ ★

Enhancing the Efficiency of State Government Through Public-Private Partnerships

One of the primary tasks of the chief executive of any organization is to assess the overall management and efficiency of its operations. Some may argue that efficiency in state government is an oxymoron. Nonetheless, thirteen Management and Efficiency (M&E) Committees, consisting of representatives from the public and private sectors, were established during my administration as governor of Colorado to improve the efficiency and responsiveness of the executive branch. Previous efforts to do so were only moderately successful because their focus had been too broad—covering too many functions at once. Our process concentrated on one area or department of government at a time.

It is particularly difficult to identify organizational problems and their solutions when in their midst. Therefore, when I took office in 1975, I asked a number of private sector leaders to aid in the in-depth examination of various departments and functions of the executive branch in order to make recommendations that would allow it to operate more efficiently.

The results of the Management and Efficiency Committees have prompted a variety of responses: action, controversy, new perspectives (on behalf of both the private sector and the public sector participants), and, in some cases, substantial changes in the management and operation of departments within the executive branch. Furthermore, the recommendations of these committees provided the impetus for several legislative actions. For example, recommendations and actions resulting from the M&E study on the Department of Labor and Employment in 1982 provided the impetus for a bill that terminated the Industrial Commission. This allowed the creation of a similar structure that possessed greater rule-making authority and was, ultimately, more effective.

The dissolution of the Industrial Commission is one example of the positive impact of the M&E studies. Yet another measure of the success of this process has been the willingness of cabinet members to have their agencies studied. In fact, for many of these individuals, receiving feedback from private sector individuals who lack strong political motives was a positive experience. This acceptance has contributed to the participatory style of management in Colorado state government. The exchange of public and private management methods and ideas was highly beneficial.

In the pages that follow, the M&E process and methodology will be outlined, and three examples will be provided to illustrate the benefits of such public-private sector cooperation. Admittedly, the studies were more effective in some areas than in others, and the outcomes were influenced by many factors. Those that affect public-private partnerships will be examined, and suggestions will be offered to maximize the positive factors and diminish the negatives.

The Role of Management and Efficiency Committees

In my first budget message to the Colorado General Assembly, I called on the bipartisan leadership to join me in establishing "a review committee of businessmen and public officials to . . . re-evaluate state operations . . . in light of the desperate need to cut frills rather than programs." The objectives of this effort were threefold: to examine and improve the management and efficiency of the state government; to develop recommendations to reduce the cost of administering necessary programs; and to encourage mutual concern by both the executive and legislative branches regarding improved management and efficiency in government.

During the course of my administration, thirteen M&E committees were established. They conducted studies on the departments of Administration, Highways, Institutions, Labor and Employment, Local Affairs, Military Affairs, Planning and Budgeting, Personnel, Regulatory Agencies, and Revenue. Two of the committees conducted cross-departmental, or horizontal, studies on critical areas: Automated Data Processing/Telecommunications and Vehicle Fleet Management.

Since the first M&E study in 1975, more than 140 committee members from the private sector and more than 155 loaned executives have examined the workings of the state government. At an unanticipated level of cooperation and commitment, top-level executives from industry, banking, real estate development, health care, and education worked with state officials and their staffs to improve governmental responsiveness.

There are several reasons for inviting representatives from the private sector to participate in improving state government. First, recognized leaders from the community at large lend impartiality and credibility to the process of setting an agenda and goals for task areas. Private sector participation also broadens the base of support for carrying out the recommendations of a study or commission. The various leaders who have participated in the effort have a stake in realizing the fruition of their efforts.

Second, by inviting industry leaders (often the most vocal critics) to participate in the process, we were able to create an openness in public management and to build relationships with key individuals who often became allies in our relations with the legislative branch. In a state where the executive branch is constitutionally weak, more allies mean more influence in legislative decisions—a prime consideration.

Finally, private sector individuals, as "outsiders," bring fresh perspectives to the process of state government. Indeed, one of the interesting and unexpected results of the M&E studies was the reaction of these participants to what they learned about state government. They gained a much better understanding of its complexities and, for the most part, a new respect for public sector officials and staff members. Upon learning of the operational constraints of state government, one committee member exclaimed to a department head: "My God, given your environment and all the layers of decision making, you're doing one helluva job!"

Representative Committee Studies

The following three examples are representative of the M&E studies. The first one, on the Department of Labor and Employment, provides a good example of how the M&E process resulted in a positive outcome. The second example concerns the Department of Institutions, in which some difficulty arose in carrying out all the committee's recommendations. Some of them were put into effect but were less beneficial than anticipated because of personnel problems or resistance to change. The final case study, on Automated Data Processing and Telecommunications, is unique in its cross-departmental approach.

The Department of Labor and Employment

The M&E study on the Department of Labor and Employment is a prime example of public-private partnership in action. Within a year and a half of the study's completion in 1982, approximately 80 percent of the committee's fifty-nine recommendations were acted on. Subsequent legislative action and other changes resulting from M&E recommendations brought the percentage to 90 percent.

The committee, which met for seven months, was well informed about labor and employment issues. It consisted of representatives from unions, labor attorneys, and industry-business leaders, all knowledgeable about labor laws. Despite the sharply divergent viewpoints on many issues, the members of this well-rounded group were skilled negotiators and were able to come to swift agreement on the recommendations.

Furthermore, the recommendations were realistic and workable. The five general areas centered on organization and accountability, personnel, automated data processing, federal-state relationships, and evaluation. When a new executive director of this department came on board, he was able to use the recommendations of the M&E study as a blueprint for improving his operations. He and other cabinet members used the recommendations as key points in their performance contracts with me.

The principal obstacle in carrying out the recommendations concerning labor and employment stemmed from staffing and funding problems that could not be addressed within the department.

The Department of Institutions

In the previous example, the implementation success rate was very high. With the Department of Institutions study, the success rate was more indirect and less quantifiable, yet some significant changes resulted from the recommendations of the M&E committee. For instance, in an effort to check inefficiencies and weaknesses, the committee strongly recommended greater centralization of authority and control within this complex department. To accomplish this, the organizational structure was modified, giving the executive director more control and better feedback from the divisions. Three new associate director positions were created (management information officer, facilities management director, and human resources officer), each of whom reported directly to the executive director. These structural changes unified the diverse divisions into a more manageable whole.

Another significant change was in the departmental planning process. The overall objectives were to integrate the process among the divisions to avoid fragmentation; to separate the planning and budgeting cycles to assure that program objectives would be the driving force, rather than budget considerations; and to encompass both programmatic and management objectives into the planning process. The executive director has found the new planning method to be a highly effective management tool. In fact, the Division of Mental Health received a National Institute of Mental Health grant for further planning based on its success.

In addition to these direct impacts, several significant changes resulted indirectly from the M&E study on the Department of Institutions. Because the M&E subcommittee on facilities management served to heighten the awareness of energy and maintenance costs, the department obtained funding for a unique way of updating energy facilities. In this creative approach, an engineering firm was hired to install a variety of energy-saving devices in state mental health centers in return for a portion of the energy cost savings. This program will cut $6.9 million from the budget over fifteen years. Net savings provided by new practices in natural gas procurement and coal conversion totaled more than $350,000 in 1985-86.

Another indirect impact of the M&E study was creation of a better relationship with the legislature. The year prior to the study, the legislature, frustrated with the Department of Institutions, introduced a bill to decentralize it. The M&E recommendations, which actually advocated more centralized authority, shed new light on the problems of the department and helped persuade legislators to work with it in a more constructive fashion. After the M&E study, the General Assembly passed a bill allocating $31 million to rebuild or replace youth corrections facilities. This was a major objective of the department's long-range master plan.

This study was unique in that the committee did not conduct a blanket-approach study of the department. Instead, the members used their expertise and experience to serve as voluntary "management consultants" to the executive director. Their aim was to focus on the formulation of solutions to major management deficiencies in the department that had been identified in previous studies of it.

ADP/Telecommunications

This was one of the more recent M&E studies to be conducted, and its impact is potentially far-reaching. State expenditures for computerized information processing exceed $60 million per year, and, though equipment costs are decreasing, expenditures in this area are likely to increase as automatic data processing (ADP) and telecommunication techniques become more widespread in the state government. Initially, the committee limited its scope to the executive branch, but at the request of the legislature extended it to include legislative information processing. This study was more intensive than most, and was distinctive because of the legislative involvement at the outset. By March 1986, more than 75 percent of the ensuing recommendations had either been acted on or were being addressed.

The state's ADP systems were such a focus of broad dissatisfaction that, at one point, the legislative Joint Budget Committee tried to eliminate the ADP budget entirely. Progress is being made, though much remains to be done in this area. The ADP Division, within the Department of Administration, is applying resources toward strategic planning, providing consulting services to various state agencies, and establishing interagency project teams to plan and utilize shared systems and resources.

The legislature, after two unsuccessful attempts, has approved the establishment of a revolving fund to finance the operation of the General Government Computer Center, which will tie computer use to agency budgets, thereby requiring prioritizing and monitoring of usage. This, along with the establishment of telecommunication service charge-backs, was recommended by the M&E committee so that both functions would be self-financing.

Statewide standards and policies for such activities as integration, word processing, and the acquisition and use of microcomputers have been established and enforced by state information systems managers. One major recommendation, to reduce the number of data centers from five to two, was not immediately effected because of resistance on the part of the departments involved. However, this could result in savings of $4 million to $6 million over a four-year period. A committee representing all parties was established to decide on how to proceed with furthering the recommendations.

In the area of telecommunications, three technical communications specialists were added to the Division of Telecommunications staff. In addition, long-range plans were defined, and a concentrated effort was made to identify and prioritize telecommunications support for all information processing needs.

The M&E Committee Process

After the first few M&E studies were conducted, the executive director of the Department of Administration (a cabinet member) assumed the duties of director for the studies. Each year, after extensive interviews with those knowledgeable about state government, he was charged with recommending to my office the two or three executive departments to be analyzed. His duties also included assembling the required staff support, which provides research, writing, and technical assistance to the M&E committees.

The committees were charged with focusing on the management, functional, and organizational aspects of state government. They were not expected to recommend changes in state policy or federal or local government responsibilities, which are beyond the scope of the executive branch. The departments were studied using three basic methodologies. Several were analyzed on a divisional basis, where subcommittees studied each subordinate division independently. Some departments were studied along functional lines that cut across divisions, some across departmental lines, and many across branches of state government. Finally, for most departments a hybrid of the two approaches was used, examining both functional and divisional aspects.

Subsequent to extensive meetings, interviews, field trips, and informational briefings on the departments, the M&E committees prepared final reports, including a series of findings and generally two types of recommendations. The first addressed the management of a particular department (for example, the need for mission statements to outline departmental goals and objectives along with other plans for reorganization of departmental functions). In general, the success rate was high for these recommendations inasmuch as they were fully within the control of the executive branch.

The second group of recommendations was more "generic" and addressed universal problems that resulted from the structure of government itself. For example, the need for statewide strategic planning was often cited, as well as an incentive compensation system for state personnel. Both of these issues were outside the jurisdiction of individual departments. Thus, the success rate of this group of recommendations was not as high as for the first group inasmuch as they were usually within the purview of the legislature and required statutory changes.

Once completed, the committees' reports were submitted to me and to the appropriate departments, which were required to comment on the potential for putting the recommendations into effect. Obstacles that precluded this included lack of legislative support or necessary funding; recommendations that were not within the purview of the department; and, subsequent to the committees' findings, changes in the departments' responsibilities, structure, or staffing that made the recommendations inappropriate. On the whole, however, departments were inclined to ' accept and carry out the committees' recommendations.

Timely action on the recommendations is one of the most critical components of the M&E process. Implementation schedules have been established, and cabinet officers have provided semiannual updates on the status of actions taken on the recommendations. In addition, committee members have assisted in the implementation process. Follow-up meetings with committee members provide for continued communication and clarification of recommendations.

Benefits of the M&E Process

In determining if the M&E process has been successful or not, one is tempted to seek an improved measure of efficiency in state government. A problem arises, however, in attempting to define such a measurement. Herbert A. Simon, in his classic work *Administrative Behavior,* notes that efficiency as a measurement of organizational objectives is the maximization of output: "The criterion of efficiency dictates that choice of alternatives which produces the largest result for the given application of resources." Although this "biggest-bang-for-the-buck" perspective may work in the private sector, it is often not applicable to the public sector. In state government, there is no bottom line of profits—no maximization of output—by which success (efficiency) can be easily measured.

Governmental efficiency, then, requires a different measure. Lewis C. Mainzer provides one such alternative in *Political Bureaucracy:* "Efficiency, in its fullest sense, involves the ability of the bureaucracy to make a contribution to the art of government." In this context, it can be argued that the M&E process has provided a positive contribution to the art of government in Colorado. A prominent reason for its success is the sustained participation of the private sector. Not only has a cadre of business leaders contributed positively to the process, but they also continue to be willing to contribute because they realize the value of the participatory style of the process. This applies to both the leaders of industry in the state as well as the executives who have volunteered or been hired to consult with the M&E committees.

Yet another measure of the success of the M&E process has been the willingness of the department directors to have their agencies studied. By and large, the directors have welcomed the fresh perspective provided by the M&E committees—strengthening the strong participatory style of management in the state government.

Moreover, the process never counted on "quick-fix" solutions to problems. Quite often, it is difficult to see immediate changes in complex organizational systems like state governments. The whole thrust of the M&E process has been to improve public management over the long term.

The M&E studies have enabled us to meet our initial objectives. The art of governing the state has been improved by creating an open and participatory style of public management. The cost of governing has been reduced in spite of the current shifts in federal spending priorities, which place more of a burden on state governments. The most difficult objective to achieve has been the cooperation of the legislature, largely because of the institutional rivalry between the sovereign branches of government: legislative and executive.

Conclusions

The use of public-private partnerships in assessing and strengthening state agencies is an excellent management tool. Actually, the business of governing is by its nature a public-private partnership. The only variable is the degree to which a governor takes advantage of the opportunities to include private sector leaders in the governing process. The following recommendations for using public-private partnerships to create efficiency in state government are based on our experiences with the Management and Efficiency studies in Colorado, but many of them come from private-sector participants in the process:

• Establish the public-private partnership early in the administration.

• Build the framework into the governing infrastructure—that is, have a pool of talent to draw upon for specific tasks.

• Identify problem areas or issues to be addressed, relate these concerns to the committee, and then give it a long leash.

• Bring in leaders from the legislature early in the process in order to obtain their input, attention, and cooperation; provide progress reports to keep them informed of the findings.

• Establish a steering committee that remains stable throughout the various studies to provide continuity and briefings for the private sector participants as well as a smooth interface between the public and private sectors.

• View the process as an opportunity for improving government rather than as an audit exercise.

• Finally, provide first-rate staff support for the committees to make their work as efficient and expeditious as possible.

Governor John H. Sununu
★ New Hampshire ★

Governor Sununu currently serves as chief of staff to President George Bush. He was the Republican governor of New Hampshire from 1983 to 1989. While governor, he served as chairman of NGA (1987-88) and was chairman of the Committee on International Trade and Foreign Relations.

A mechanical engineer by vocation, Governor Sununu received his bachelor's, master's, and doctorate degrees from the Massachusetts Institute of Technology. His career has traversed both public and private pursuits, including roles as a founder of a private engineering firm, a professor of engineering at Tufts University, and a state legislator.

His remarks as a gubernatorial fellow were made at Duke University on October 28, 1985.

★ ★ ★ ★ ★

Reality and Perception in Gubernatorial Management

A revolution is taking place today in the government and public processes. First, public demand for accountability of performance is placing an ever-increasing obligation on public institutions such as state government. Second, the background of some governors is nontraditional—that is, outside the political spectrum. I probably fall into that category myself, though I did serve one term in the legislature and had some involvement in local politics. But otherwise I and some other governors probably conform to the Founding Fathers' concept of politicians who have an avocation outside of state government and are willing to devote some time to public service and then quickly return to the "real world."

Whatever the backgrounds of governors, their efforts involve both reality and perception. They need to determine what the key principles are in trying to deal with an entity such as a state government and seeking to make it fulfill what people's perception is that it ought to be doing: providing traditional state services as efficiently as possible. Governors like to think that is what they are doing. Sometimes they accomplish it, sometimes they do not. Every once in a while, they are lucky and perception and reality coincide.

The reality of what governors are trying to accomplish is the definition of state policy. They run on a platform, they make commitments to the public, they say what they plan to accomplish, they specify what they hope to change or retain. In essence, these are a set of promises defining a policy that must be translated into specific gubernatorial and/or legislative actions. The next, and more difficult, step is to convert that statement of policy into a plan and agenda—a series of actions that turn policy into reality.

Perception is a strong tool in helping shape that reality—to fulfill the commitments that were made during the election process and in the statement of personal philosophy. Governors must create an image of credibility among the population they serve. In terms of dealing with the legislature, they must establish a relationship that is quite often based on perception, though the interactions sometimes take place through third parties. In the process of dealing with the legislature, quite often governors utilize the public perception of themselves as a vehicle to influence the legislature to deal with particular issues. Sometimes conflict results. Governors want to appear to be in control, and yet in certain situations a little lack of control or predictability is also an asset. On the other hand, they must not allow themselves to be stereotyped to the degree that they are viewed as being so much in control that they become absolutely predictable. These are the ingredients of the perception that needs to be cultivated.

In establishing policies, discipline is required. Many governors assume office and want to do everything all at once for everybody. In my own case, exercising self-discipline, I established a very limited agenda. In fact, during my first term, it was limited to one item: reestablishing the fiscal integrity of the state of New Hampshire.

My predecessor had assumed office in a state that was proud of its fiscal structure. It had always maintained a triple A bond rating and had always operated with a solid budget surplus. Although it levied neither sales nor income taxes, it had delivered all the necessary services and was proud of their quality. During the four years that my predecessor served, two two-year terms, the state was twice downgraded in bond rating and built up a significant deficit. Furthermore, virtually all the political leaders in the state felt that sales and income taxes might need to be adopted to solve the fiscal crisis. I had made the commitment to manage the state efficiently without these taxes and established my limited agenda for that purpose.

Establishing a limited agenda places tremendous pressure on governors, their staffs, and all the constituencies that helped elect them. These groups make their own particular interests as much or more a priority as other items. A tough line must be drawn. For example, staff people may not have an interest in state finances, but may want to place their priorities in such fields as social services or education at the top of the agenda.

Once governors have selected and controlled their limited agendas, the next step is to move to the perception side of the issue and clarify in the most advantageous way the nature of that agenda. They may choose to make it visible in its entirety or just certain portions of it—preferably selecting those items that promise success and deemphasizing the potentially troublesome ones. In any case, part of the perception in trying to marshal resources within the state to assist you is to point out what you feel is important. Of course, that creates vulnerability because opponents are provided with valuable knowledge. That factor is, therefore, part of the balance in trying to decide what ought to be defined in terms of the perception and the reality of the agenda. The two lists or portions of them may coincide or may differ slightly.

Once the agenda is set, governors must understand that they can act only within the reality of the existing environment. They need to try to sense public moods in seeking to coalesce their influence on the legislature. Governors should also have a feeling for what the legislature might do or not do, as well as an understanding of the economic environment that exists within the state, the region, and the nation. The ground rules, the limitations on what might be possible within a state, are clearly a part of establishing the scenario for action.

For example, historically the people of New Hampshire have opposed sales and income taxes. This is a reality when dealing with the fiscal condition of that state. Of course, when such limitations exist, an effort can be made to change the environment. That environment, including public opinion, may be influenced by education, by governors using the power of their office. But, for the most part, that is a difficult and time-consuming project. Proper assessment of what can be done in the available time frame and the environment involved during that period is mandatory. Here is a case in point. Many states got into trouble in the late seventies and early eighties by assuming the straight-line theory of revenue projection: extending a line from the last two years. Growth was extrapolated on the basis of two good years, which were followed by a relatively strong economic downturn.

In dealing with the fiscal situation in New Hampshire, I tried to determine what the economic situation was going to be nationwide and regionally as well as within the state. Upon discovering that the projections for our state, as well as others, were informal and weak, my staff assembled data generated by at least a dozen economic surveys and created our own model based on the history of what had happened in New Hampshire relative to what had been predicted in the past nationally. The correlation was reasonably good. A number of people were surprised with our prediction that the state was going to perform significantly better economically than New England as a whole, and that New England was going to surpass the nation.

Frankly, I played "You Bet Your Budget" and designed a budget that was responsive to the most likely economic scenario for the state. Some safety valves were included. The budget was designed to deal with a significant crisis in the state based on the best available estimates of the economic climate and environment during the succeeding two years. Because of the two-year budgeting cycle, we needed a sense of what would be happening over the longer term, rather than just the next six or twelve months. That may seem like almost a given in many situations, but it is surprising how many states and even businesses do not acquire such data.

What are my reasons for dwelling on the budget and my state's achievements in this field? First, it was the most significant accomplishment during my first term. Second, I think the budget is probably the strongest tool for policy determination and implementation that governors have. They should do whatever is necessary to maintain control of the budget preparation and budget legislation cycle. There is no better means for policy definition and policy implementation.

In order to carry out policy, certain steps are required that either by virtue of law or of administrative rules or executive orders create the regulatory environment under which that policy will be turned into reality. I am convinced that the major change that is taking place in terms of the way states do business is the same one that is taking place in the private sector: the understanding that acquiring, analyzing, and utilizing information effectively is a potent vehicle. In my judgment, most state governments have not properly recognized and practiced this.

The best way for governors to control the budget cycle is to know more about what is going on in all departments than do the heads of these departments and then require those individuals to know more about what is transpiring in all their divisions than their directors. Without a doubt that takes extra effort and demands the kind of people who are not necessarily available full time within state government. New governors sometimes have to reach beyond traditional resources for the help that is necessary.

In my particular case, New Hampshire in 1982, I had to assemble a team of people from the private sector to help restructure a budget in the ninety-day period between the election and the presentation of the budget the second week of February in the legislative session. The quality of those personnel is important. Their major assets are their experience in budgeting, whether it was in the public or private sectors, and their understanding that institutional budgets are traditionally made in a simplistic way: adding 20 percent to last year's budget and hoping that the cut is only to a 10 percent increase.

I was chairman of the finance committee at Tufts University for a while. The best preparation for the politics of preparing a state budget is experience with a university budget because of the strong similarity in the procedures of allocation of resources. The difference between what is perceived as a department that is operating efficiently and the reality of that department long ago created for itself an interrelationship and myriad of accounts and account numbers in which resources for rainy days can be squirrelled away and utilized at the discretion of either the dean or the department head. The same thing happens in state government, but it is sometimes a little bit harder to find.

In terms of formulating a budget, let me say again that the usual assumption is that the information being used in state government is the best available. But it is not. In virtually no institution is the best set of information available being used, though many people perceive it to be adequate. In just about every institution, there is room for significant improvement. In New Hampshire's particular case when I assumed office, the opportunity was tremendous.

It was obvious during the second term of my predecessor that financial times were tough. The nation was experiencing a slight economic downturn, and the estimated revenues of various states were below what was expected. At the same time, not only were expenditures continuing along at the rate people had anticipated, but also in many cases the downturn itself put pressure for additional expenditures, such as those in the welfare area.

In many states, the time lag between determining what is actually spent program by program between the time that expenditure actually takes place and the time it is reported to those whose responsibility it is to make policy is not measured in days and sometimes not in weeks but in months. That kind of a lag creates serious instabilities.

I took office after campaigning against an incumbent who claimed that the budget was balanced. At the beginning of the campaign, a $5 million deficit was projected; on election day, it was $8 million to $10 million. Within a week after being elected and gaining access to some more information as governor-elect, I found it was going to be close to $20 million. After I instituted a 4 percent across-the-board cut and after all purchases were frozen that could be deferred until the next year, we ended up with a $44 million deficit. And we were not sure of that until three or four months after we closed the books on June 30. Policy decisions cannot be made with that kind of lag in crucial revenue and expenditure information.

Although state governments have as much need for quality information as the private sector, they have often failed to utilize what technology offers them in terms of data processing and tying it together to provide common access by policymakers to the information that is available. New Hampshire has established an integrated financial system focused on a common data base that includes virtually every transaction, whether it be a purchase order or a payment voucher or a hiring of a consultant or a purchase of liquor inventory for the state liquor stores. That data base is monitored by management programs that coalesce performance division by division and department by department on the basis of fund sources, or in terms of personnel, and so on. The data base is accessible through the governor's personal office computer, which makes possible downloading the entire data structure onto a hard disk and operating on it with office spread-sheet programs in order to produce in effect a pro forma daily closing. Of course, that is only approximate because of the kind of approximations that are necessary with some of the revenues and expenditures. But the system is at least an order of magnitude better than it was before, and anticipated improvements are expected to provide data that are close to being representative of the reality that is ultimately sought for the decision making that produces good policy.

A strange situation in New Hampshire hampered my budget preparation. Under the system, the governor is not able to appoint all department heads right after election. Most of them are appointed for four-year terms, though the governor serves for two years. Therefore, I had to put a budget together on the basis of information being provided by departments whose chairmen or commissioners were not my appointees and who therefore represented both the philosophy and agenda of my predecessor, which were very different from mine.

Aided by the team of people we brought in from the outside, about seventy-five of the ninety days we used to prepare the budget were devoted to establishing the assumptions on which the budget would be based rather than on monetary allotments. Ignoring agency requests for additional funds per se over the preceding year, we concentrated on program goals, the justification for them, and the best way to accomplish them. On the basis of our model for the economic structure of the state, without ever having discussed how much money was going to be allocated to certain departments, we finally agreed upon the ground rules. Then, literally in the last fifteen days, we put the budget together on a line-by-line basis. In every case, issue by issue, we struggled to identify the existing condition, to define the correlation of changes from it to changes in either economic structure or other quantifiable parameters that would either come from our model or from the best assumptions that we might establish. On the basis of this approach, we restructured a budget from scratch. This was not the traditional method in New Hampshire or in many other states—but it was a method I believe ought to be used in the future.

Another problem was that even though the legislature was controlled by my own party, I had to convince its members that my approach was reasonable. In the difficult times that prevailed at that time in the state, in the crisis conditions that existed, it was easy to persuade the legislators that they ought to let me take the responsibility for the budget. By testifying on its details myself, something that had not been done in the past in the state, I reinforced the perception, which turned out to be the reality, not only of the legislature, but also of the public, that this was my budget. That made it easier for the legislature to approve it. Even when perception and reality coincide, you need to work on the perception part as well.

The approximately $2 billion budget was passed for the biennium with about $3 million worth of change—as small an amount as anybody ever remembered in the state. The only major change other than the expenditure side of $3 million was that the legislature felt I was underestimating revenues and persuaded me to generate some additional ones. This was probably just political face-saving. Our original revenue estimates were right on the mark, but thanks to the legislature's insistence, we closed the biennium on June 30, 1985, with about a $47 million surplus. And we moved up two notches in bond rating.

The advantage of having limited my agenda to a single item was that this allowed my administration to focus all our efforts and resources on that goal; and in the eyes of the public, I fulfilled all the commitments I had made. The public perception of my being able to make a commitment on what appeared to be an impossible task and then accomplishing it created strong credibility and political capital that enabled me to deal with some of the other crucial state issues.

Just as perception and reality differ in politics, so too do strategy and tactics. They differ from state to state and from public office to public office. But the calendar basically determines the distinction between tactical and strategic efforts. Because of the two-year gubernatorial term in New Hampshire, it was almost impossible for governors to receive political credit for long-term strategic decisions. Unfortunately, if they are to do their job well, they have to include in their agendas some of those long-range requirements, whether or not they receive any credit.

In my own case, an example is the energy situation in New England— one of the reasons I became involved in politics. The U.S. Congress thinks that an energy policy is a gas and oil policy, but it is much more than that. In New England the energy issue is electrical energy production. The reality is that the region will soon have shortfalls in deliverable electrical energy capacity—even if two controversial projects, Millstone III in Connecticut and Seabrook in New Hampshire, and the hydropower being purchased from Canada all come on line exactly as projected. Seabrook is a highly emotional tactical issue whose strategic political benefit I will never realize, but it had to be dealt with in a constructive way. The easy route would have been to emotionalize the issue and not endorse it on the basis of the political dangers. Frankly, I did not feel comfortable with that; I have long advocated that this country needs to understand that it has an energy shortage in a number of areas—electricity being the most visible one—and that nuclear facilities have to be built.

During my first term, other than the budget, the most difficult public issue was the Seabrook power plant. Its principal builder, a New Hampshire company named the Public Service of New Hampshire, was tottering on the verge of bankruptcy. It obviously did not understand that in order to build a nuclear power plant you had to have built one before, at least in today's milieu. In constructing any major energy or industrial facility, the complexity of the regulatory structure and the difficulty of dealing with it is such that experience in such an endeavor is required. Although that seems to suggest that nobody will ever be able to build anything new, the fact is that a company can buy that experience—not through consultants but through in-house management. But the company failed to comprehend that.

As a member of the private sector before I became governor, I had urged that company to make an investment in quality management, but this suggestion had gone unheeded. However, because of the regulatory power possessed by the governor of New Hampshire, I soon gained new wisdom in the company's eyes. Exercising what I believe is one of the most underused assets of a governor—persuasion—I finally was able to convince the company to hire an experienced project manager. It recruited Bill Derekson, who had just brought Florida's Saint Lucy II plant on line, on schedule, and generally within budget. The difference in the project management since then has been overwhelming.

Yet I did not benefit politically from my strategic decision, but carried a political burden. However, I have no regret over the part I played in advancing the project. Nobody knew whether it was going to be successful or whether my involvement and continued support for it was a political plus or minus. According to the polls, it was a minus. Everybody in the state said it was a volatile political issue. My predecessor had been elected by emotionalizing it against his predecessor in 1978. Not only did the public think that it was a critical issue, but they also certainly knew my stance, which did not represent the majority point of view.

This situation can be linked to the budget issue. In that case, I had made a commitment to undertake a financial task that was perceived to be difficult and had delivered a budget that was very much contrary to general wisdom. Because of the credibility and the political capital thus gained, the public was willing to be patient with my approach to the energy issue. The perception that is created by the success of the limited agenda is a valuable tool to use in dealing with other difficult matters.

Based on my experience, I believe that governors must not debase their personal styles to match those of other governors. They must rely on their strongest assets. Sometimes others may perceive them as advantages, sometimes as disadvantages. The best use must be made of the talents and style that are the most comfortable for the individual. Some people argue that the responsibility for digesting large amounts of data and deciding on courses of action can be transferred to others who pass on this information to you. However, I think that hoping others will do the detailed work results in the incapability to match the style and the strategy to your own capabilities and personal intuition. In effect, crucial decisions are delegated to somebody else.

I am also convinced from my experiences as governor and from visiting companies as a consultant that the best way to find a solution to a difficult problem is to get back as close as possible to basic data before the bias of processing is built into it. Everyone has biases, and even the decision as to what data to examine is in itself a bias. In making decisions, governors ought to know enough about the system to dictate the data they want generated and examined, to define its processing, and to determine the kind and context of its presentation at each level along the way. Relegation of these functions to somebody else also passes on control of the basic assumptions as well as the ensuing decisions. Examination of the data after they have passed through half a dozen layers of this process results in a predetermined decision. The system and those within it make the decision by selecting, processing, biasing, and packaging the information.

Some chief executives feel that their style of government is to overhaul the entire system so that every person in it reflects their philosophy, their personal bias, and the direction that they would like to take. They may be successful in this approach, but I do not feel comfortable in being able to identify those inclinations in every person I have working for me.

Therefore, personnel selection is critical. A hierarchy of management requires transferral of responsibility and obligation to others. But recruiting capable personnel in the public sector is very much different in one sense from the private sector. That is, talented people with the kind of experience that corresponds to your agenda and who are politically sensitive are needed. Sometimes this means recruiting somebody with a little less experience, a little bit less talent, but a little political sensitivity. In the long run, political capital is wasted in dealing with the fire started by the politically insensitive.

Experiences and skills that individuals from the private sector bring are very important in government, especially in today's context. In my opinion, they possess two major attributes, the first of which is a background more committed to measured performance—determined on the basis of output rather than input parameters. Too many people in public service measure their importance or the quality of their efforts by the size of their budget or the number of people who work for them.

The second attribute of private sector personnel is quite often not only a willingness but in fact a desire to serve only for a short period of time. They tend to stress quality of performance instead of longevity of service. This is equally true of governors. In my own case, the worst thing that could happen is being sent back to the private sector—not an unpleasant alternative. I like my department heads to feel the same way. We assumed office to accomplish our agenda and are willing to demonstrate some sensitivity in achieving its goals. You do not want bulls in a china shop, but you also do not want people who are so afraid of the first press criticism that they hurry to change their policy lest they become politically unpopular. These are some of the major assets of personnel from the private sector.

Another major aspect of personnel management for governors is that they should not underestimate the importance of appointments at all levels of government. In seeking to influence the hiring structure, most governors concentrate on commissioners and department and agency heads without spending any time at all on looking at positions that may be three, four, and five layers down—though policies are involved at those levels that are very significant to governors. Within my state, the Office of Alcohol and Drug Abuse Prevention is a number of layers down in the hierarchy from the commissioner of health and welfare. But this was an area I felt strongly about, where I believed some major changes in policy were required, especially the establishment of educational programs for offenders and school children. So I became closely involved in that appointment and was able to recruit a highly qualified individual from the private sector who had strong experience in substance abuse programs.

Another similar step I took resulted from my dissatisfaction with the federally funded state job training program. My feeling was that those funds ought to reflect policies and programs that matched private sector needs in my state. It is folly to train somebody for a job that does not exist. To make sure that individual and industrial needs were coordinated, I felt an executive director was needed for that program. Although this might have been considered as a minor appointment, I spent some time on it.

My basic point is that gubernatorial agendas contain important though minor elements that would normally be delegated to somebody else where governors should become involved. In the long run, in many of those areas, the return on the investment of time is significant. The alternative is exerting effort either to redirect people who have a slightly different perspective or to monitor their actions.

One other area that is crucial for governors to understand is that states respond to trends, events, and conditions beyond their own borders. What happens in New Hampshire's economy is determined not just by the governor, the legislature, and the state bureaucracy, but to a great extent by what is happening regionally and nationally. Conversely, I think governors are beginning to appreciate—certainly through the National Governors' Association—their capacity to speak out on issues and to influence national policy. Another vehicle for doing so is their unique power to influence their state congressional delegations.

Here is a case in point concerning the need for governors to participate personally in some dealings with the federal government. I and many others in the state believed the federal policy in funding programs for the elderly was very counterproductive. Federal funds could be provided only to programs in a nursing home setting, not to home-based assistance programs. What is more likely to break up families than a situation that forces children to put their parents in nursing homes because they cannot afford to provide some of the special services needed at home? What is less efficient in terms of health care than burdening the family with some of the responsibilities that are paid for in a nursing home setting? To change this situation, a federal waiver was required, which I obtained by lobbying the secretary of health and human services.

Another topic about which I feel strongly is education—a major political issue today that is of concern to all governors. I find myself in a bit of a quandary. It is sort of paradoxical: someone like myself who has made a living for sixteen years as a faculty member taking positions that disturb people in the education community. Education is important in this country in terms of public expenditures. It is the largest single one on the state and local levels. Not only should that money be spent efficiently, but it also represents a crucial step in the nation's effort to be more competitive in world markets.

Too many people want to talk about education in terms of price tags rather than performance parameters. Most legislative debates about education stress comparisons of expenditures. That context needs to be changed—particularly by those educational lobbyists who are trying to take advantage of this country's willingness to fund the improvement of education as a mechanism to serve a separate agenda that is more concerned with revenues for certain elements of the educational community than with the quality of education.

The argument is made that an increase in teachers' salaries will automatically enhance the quality of education. As a former faculty member, I would love to have salaries increased. But I contend that this is not the best investment for improvement in quality of education, and at the primary and secondary level it is probably the worst indicator. The highest teaching salaries in the country are in New York City, Boston, Detroit, and Los Angeles. Because of other social and economic conditions, part of those salaries are for teaching and part for "combat pay."

The emphasis should move from teachers' salaries to quantitative performance measurements, or parameters. Three of these are Scholastic Aptitude Test (SAT) scores, the number of students taking the test, and the percentage of those who go on to college. An absolutely negative correlation exists between these criteria and teachers' salaries because other parameters dominate what happens in an educational system much more than salary does—especially socioeconomic conditions in particular communities.

The point is that I think the most important way to improve education is to reestablish a climate and attitude among teachers, parents, and students that favor accountability, or measurement. Once the decision is made at the policy level concerning the appropriate measurements, then the mechanisms should be instituted to determine quantitatively what the results are. This approach should mark the beginning of an information structure, or data base, that will stimulate more effective investments in education.

As one who comes out of the education system, I can tell you I do not know of any profession that has done less in improving productivity and quality. Some of the views and taboos of teachers and educational policymakers must be altered. For example, the top mathematicians are not needed to teach mathematics or the best physicists to teach physics. What is required are good teachers who happen to be knowledgeable about the two subjects. Contending that the schools must compete in salaries with industry to obtain the best technical people for teaching the sciences and mathematics is a serious mistake—one that many states are making.

In conclusion, I would like to point out some of my achievements as governor and a few recent accomplishments of my state of New Hampshire. Despite the absence of sales and income taxes and while retaining the lowest rate of local plus state taxes per thousand dollars of income of any state in the country, we have constructed and refurbished major facilities for prisoners, the mentally ill, and the developmentally disabled. In terms of its institutions, this has involved virtually a complete restructuring of the capital assets of the state.

In the field of education, the state has achieved good results on the performance parameter end. The state university system has one of the highest ratios of out-of-state applications to positions available in the nation. During several recent years, New Hampshire has had the highest rate of growth of personal income of any state in the country.

Many of these accomplishments are attributable to the state's traditional emphasis on keeping as many of the governing and service processes at the lowest level of government as possible. This strong reliance on the communities is the key to the quality that has been attained. But even beyond that, the state has always insisted on holding its officials strictly accountable. The two-year gubernatorial term is reflective of the constructive relationship that exists between the elected officials and the people of the state. Another indicator is the four-hundred-person legislature—the highest in number and the highest ratio of legislators per population in the nation. These factors have created a climate of responsiveness and contact between the elected officials and the electorate that creates an excellent feedback loop. Indeed, the quality of this loop distinguishes New Hampshire from many other states. And it is one of the factors that made serving as governor of the state a challenging and interesting assignment for me.

★ ★ ★ ★ ★

Endnotes

1. The New Federalism proposed by President Nixon and President Reagan would decentralize political power and restructure governmental relationships on a grand scale, generally devolving funds and responsibilities downward, from the federal government to state and local governments. The federal block grant is a principal instrument of New Federalism.

2. Edwin Meese III, attorney general; James A. Baker III, secretary of the treasury; David A. Stockman, director of the Office of Management and Budget; and Richard S. Williamson, assistant to the president for intergovernmental affairs.

3. In its 1962 ruling in *Baker v. Carr*, the U.S. Supreme Court broke a long-standing precedent against federal court involvement in legislative apportionment problems. The case involved a challenge to the constitutionality of the legislative arrangement of the Tennessee state legislature, which had not reapportioned itself since 1901 despite a requirement in the state constitution that the legislature be reapportioned every ten years according to the number of qualified voters.

4. Robert Moses participated in many state government activities in New York, especially in the reorganization of state government and the development of state park, public works, and welfare programs. He was chief of staff in 1919-20 of the New York State Reconstruction Commission, appointed by Governor Alfred E. Smith.

5. See note 1.

6. *The New York Times*, April 27, 1984.

7. The Dixon-Yates contract between the Atomic Energy Commission and a private power combine provoked sharp controversy in 1954 between respective congressional advocates of public versus private ownership of power plants.

8. James Hagerty, press secretary; Sherman Adams, chief of staff; Wilton Persons, special assistant; and Jerry Morgan, deputy assistant.

9. Maurice Stans, secretary of commerce in the Nixon administration and subsequent treasurer of the Committee to Reelect the President.

10. H.R. 1720, a welfare reform bill sponsored by Senator Daniel P. Moynihan, was signed into law in 1986 (P.L. 100-485). The law requires states to implement work and training programs for welfare mothers and to offer welfare payment to poor two-parent families. The law also strengthens enforcement of child support payment and extends child care and medical benefits to families whose parents have left welfare rolls for jobs.

11. See note 3.

12. *Time*, vol 116, no. 16 (October 20, 1980), p. 33.

13. See note 1.

14. A unitary tax treats corporate subsidiaries collectively as a single unit; it is levied on a portion of the entire unit's profits.

★ ★ ★ ★ ★

Works Cited

Bowman, Ann, and Richard Kearney. *The Resurgence of States.* Englewood Cliffs, N.J.: Prentice Hall, 1986.

Broder, David S. *The Party's Over: The Failure of Politics in America.* New York: Harper and Row, 1972.

Carney, James D. "Downsizing Government: Iowa's Challenge." *Journal of State Government,* July/August 1987.

Fuller, John G. *We Almost Lost Detroit.* New York: Reader's Digest Press, 1975.

Goodlad, John I. *A Place Called School: Prospects for the Future.* New York: McGraw-Hill, 1983.

The Holmes Group. *Tomorrow's Teachers.* East Lansing, Mich.: The Holmes Group, November 1986.

Mainzer, Lewis C. *Political Bureaucracy.* Glenview, Ill.: Foresman Scott, 1973.

Naisbitt, John. *Megatrends.* New York: Warner Books, 1982.

National Commission on Excellence in Education. *A Nation at Risk: The Imperative for Educational Reform.* Washington, D.C.: U.S. Government Printing Office, 1983.

National Governors' Association. *Time for Results: The Governors' 1991 Report on Education*. Washington, D.C.: National Governors' Association, 1986.

Osborne, David. *Laboratories of Democracy*. Boston: Harvard Business School Press, 1988.

Reedy, George. *Twilight of the Presidency*. New York: New American Library, 1987.

Sabato, Larry. *Goodbye to Good-Time Charlie: The American Governorship Transformed*. Washington, D.C.: Congressional Quarterly Press, 1983.

Sanford, Terry. *Storm Over the States*. New York: McGraw-Hill, 1967.

Schlesinger, Arthur. *The Imperial Presidency*. Boston: Houghton Mifflin, 1973.

Simon, Herbert A. *Administrative Behavior*. New York: Free Press, 1976.

Sizer, Theodore R. *Horace's Compromise: The Dilemma of the American High School*. Boston: Houghton Mifflin, 1984.

Task Force on Teaching as a Profession. *A Nation Prepared: Teachers for the 21st Century*. New York: Carnegie Forum on Education and the Economy, 1986.

Tippett, Frank. *The States: United They Fell*. Cleveland, Ohio: World Publishing Company, 1967.

★ ★ ★ ★ ★

About the Editor

Dr. Robert D. Behn is a professor of public policy and the director of The Governors Center at Duke University. He has been at Duke University since 1983. Behn has a bachelor's degree in physics from Worcester Polytechnic Institute and a master's degree in engineering and a doctorate in decision and control from Harvard University. His extensive public and private experience includes working on the staff of Massachusetts Governor Francis W. Sargent as assistant for urban affairs. He also held positions with the Council for Excellence in Government, Harvard University, The Ripon Society, The Rand Corporation, the Lincoln Laboratory, the Association for Public Policy Analysis and Management, and the Public Policy and Management Program for Case/Course Development.

About the National Governors' Association

The National Governors' Association, founded in 1908 as the National Governors' Conference, is the instrument through which the nation's governors collectively influence the development and implementation of national policy and apply creative leadership to state issues. The association's members are the governors of the fifty states, the commonwealths of the Northern Mariana Islands and Puerto Rico, and the territories of American Samoa, Guam, and the Virgin Islands. The association works closely with the administration and Congress on state-federal policy issues in its offices in the Hall of the States in Washington, D.C. The association serves as a vehicle for sharing knowledge of innovative programs among the states and provides technical assistance and consultant services to governors on a wide range of management and policy issues.